Welcome to Leicester

Edited by Emma Lee and Ambrose Musiyiwa

First Published 2016 by Dahlia Publishing Ltd
6 Samphire Close, Hamilton, Leicester, LE5 1RW
http://www.dahliapublishing.co.uk/
ISBN 9780995634404

Printed by Grosvenor Group

A CIP catalogue record for this book is available from The British
Library.

Contents

Introduction

In 2015, Leicester City Council erected signs along all entry points into the city with the legend,

> *Welcome to*
> *LEICESTER*
> *Historic City*

This led to a conversation on Facebook about how the signs didn't give any real sense of just how exciting Leicester's past, present and future are. Leicester is the site of one of the oldest known urban settlements in Britain, has made a huge contribution to the development of the English language, and has been at the centre of movements such as those that led to the development of parliamentary democracy in Britain, votes for women and the abolishment of the Atlantic Slave Trade. While, following Leicester's miraculous Premiership win, another set of signs were put up to along most major roads within in the city itself to celebrate that victory, it still didn't show that Leicester is now currently one of the most plural and diverse cities anywhere in the world.

Shortly after that discussion, we set up the Facebook group, Welcome to Leicester, to explore if it would be possible to put together an anthology of poems which would explore Leicester's past, present and future and what the city means to different people. Leicester is like a family member: its faults are acknowledged but it's still loved.

We put out a call for submissions through social media

channels like Facebook and twitter, emails to writing groups and schools as well as regional media outlets. We asked what message would you give to others about Leicester? What stories would you tell? We wanted grit and glitter, compassion and communication.

We also sent out invites to the five cities in other parts of the world that are twinned with Leicester - Chongqing in China; Krefeld in Germany; Masaya in Nicaragua; Rajkot in India; and Strasbourg in France - as well as to the seven towns that are also called Leicester - Leicester, Sierra Leone; Leicester, North Carolina; Leicester, Massachusetts; Leicester, Vermont; Leicester, New York; Leicester (village), New York; and Leicester Township, Clay County, Nebraska.

In all, we received 182 poems. From these, we selected 90 poems because of how the poems worked on their own and as part of Welcome to Leicester. We made sure that each poem that was included in the anthology didn't duplicate another. We hope you will enjoy reading the collection of poems that are in this anthology as much as we did.

We also hope that Welcome to Leicester will be part of the conversation the city is having with itself and with others about all the things Leicester is and can be.

Emma Lee and Ambrose Musiyiwa

Kaleidoscope

"Life isn't about finding yourself. Life is about creating
yourself." George Bernard Shaw

The place is alive in a kaleidoscope mellay of patterns
and shapes that fill the senses,
every day and night.
The sights and sounds pounce
like a mathematical puzzle or mandala
from every open space,
at the King Power stadium
to the local market and smells
like habanero and cinnamon disperse
in the Caribbean festival air.

Every person
can create the kaleidoscope,
as each new pattern
is discovered. Life isn't about
finding yourself in the candela
of misshapen dead ends
but in the patterns of life, in a city of colours
where a new identity can be created.

David Holloway

Leicester

You are a legend of cities.
You embody all the glories of ages.
My sweetest sparrow, my precious harp.
My tears splattered my cheeks as I travelled in exile.
But here, I dream of violets, remember perfumes,
birds soaring through clouds.
Your throne is still engraved like royal mirrors
of all times and places.
Your love still grows within your Roman walls.
You light a flame of love in my heart which will never
        fade.
Still your tune dances in my veins.

How I longed for such a home
like Summer waits for rain.
People see me as a refugee.
But I am a free bird, nestling in your grass.
I have nothing, only love and rain, but I'm richest
under your warm heart, drawing me to your depths.
In the fire of your love, even my blood becomes
        wine.
You and me are love until deep sleep, sleep-moon.
You are all letters, all language.
You are the end, the start of my journey.

Malka Al-Haddad

her green lap
Spinney Hill Park

spread to the edges of the park
endless to my eyes of eighteen months

and my delighting feet sloshed through
the dew-slick flood of grass

that poured down the hill to beach
on the tarmac slab where hung the box on chains

dropped into which and launched
I laughed and strained to clutch the wary birds

and offer them my first joy of my first knowing
of the first time of the world.

Paul Lee
title from Milton's "Song on a May Morning"

Henna On Her Hands

For the people of Belgrave with whom I lived

She will wear her lemon chiffon sari
with an ochre blouse and petticoat.
She will walk barefoot,
letting whispers of silk kiss her ankles.
Bells sing in a late sunlight.

She will tread over sandalwood
and jasmine to the old women
to have henna painted on her palms,
on white porcelain feet, as a blessing.
They will fuss her paleness.
In the baked red kitchen clay
they unveil a secrecy, a pattern,
stitching it with paste vines, leaves,
earth flowers until roots stick,
until she breathes the ancient.

They talk with women words
blushing the room in an innocence
whilst she washes in herbs, anoints herself
with oil from a cracked jar,
playing with another's skin.

Bracelets sing on busy wrists
and, happy with her hidden sister, Daxia
gives a small vermillion bindi
for her head as a seal, a sign, an eye
for the nine day dance.

Then let us take the garba pot
and spin each other's skirts
around a wheel, an earth, finding
its difficult, delicate rhythm.
We hold each other in the round

wearing one another;
none so very different.

Dawn Bauling

Castle Gardens

A city's life enhancer
of sights and sounds
the drone and throbbing
along the ribboned highway
meandering paths
and green crust infested waterway.

Rain falling as a silk wash
on half opened eyes
as the four smoothly glide
white tipped oars dipping,
dripping as they pass by.

A black, locked, iron gate
the sweet scent of lilac petals
as they nod through the rusted bars
beyond, brick and stone
rise up from shackled
dungeons deep below.

Striding quickly away past trunks
of roughened bark whose very roots
are set to catch the dreamer
is a cloud of yellow fronded
spikes growing tall inside
a crazy paved surround.

Beyond black timbered arch
a place of Holy worship
whose ancient carved walls
offer comfort from within
nearby, a spreading horse chestnut
shelters diverse standing stones with inscriptions.

Time is slowly moving on
and the tree lined street fills
with a bright dappled light
a moment of sheer joy overcomes
as the past blends with the present
when around a corner
a group of waste skips
pour out their vinee spice and
winged angels
take flight
over all.

Muir Sperrings

Late Night, Granby Street

The down-and-outs sleep in their doorways
As dusk dyes the town ochre-blonde
In choirs of slow sleepy snoring
The late buses murmur their song.

The cash-machine drunks on the pavements
Meander in question-mark queues
To eat by the old canal railings
Cold ships wrapped in blankets of news.

The buskers have left in the subway
Guitar strings and rivers of coins
And folk-songs to sing to the drum-play
Stiletto girls leave in the void.

The street lamps are paler than roses
Dry-pressed in a photograph book
And as the old century closes
They wane in the stale city dust.

Past the radio towers and pylons
And under the crumbling bridge
Past the station lights' flare and the night song
Of gossiping rooks in the wind

Past a tired town weary of wishing
That sleeps in its stained russet bed
A tremulous star in the distance
Descends to its fathomless death.

But as the last night train is leaving
A sleepless child stares at the sky
And blesses its passing with feeling
Of hope beyond transient life.

Julia Wood

Secular Hall

From its façade, you could mistake it for a chapel,
secular yet another Christian schism.

But *libertas* is engraved in the stone, high up,
and in niches beneath it, busts of Thomas Paine,

Socrates, Voltaire and, bizarrely, Jesus,
stare across a city centre road

at supermarket, discount store and pub.
Taped to its window, a sign proclaims

Hands that help are better than lips that pray
ignoring that some do both,

and that the battle it urges is long won,
having left fewer lips that pray, few hands that help.

Paul Lee

Finding My Way

I didn't come here by choice: I was happy in London.
It was my roommate's sister's fault
asking if *her* roommate could stay with us.

Thirty-six hours in this woman's company
and she and I are walking from St Margaret's
at midnight, the city unfolding like a dream,

any sense of direction willingly surrendered
to tramlines beneath the tarmac, leading
to a bed we feel we've shared many times before.

She points out a Roman wall in the glow
of a Holiday Inn, the stone where a king
dashed his brains returning from battle,

the sewing machine factory where her brother
is an apprentice, the printing press her grandfather
worked at, her uncle following in his footsteps.

When I return a week later, on the first train
of the day out of St Pancras, I need an A-to-Z
to find my way down Granby Street, momentarily

distracted by Cheapside, then up High Street,
over Richard III Bridge to Tudor Road,
armed with jam, fresh bread and flowers.

Charles G Lauder Jr

The view from Marks and Spencers

Ground Floor:

Faceless mannequins
stand in awkward poses,
their not-quite-noses
pressed firm against the glass
staring out into Gallowtree Gate.

Buzzards swarm in rainbow anoraks,
eyes down, scanning for crow's flight path.
Bagpipes chime with panpipes,
songs of the world drifting
between the Saturday morning traffic.

First Floor:

Slatted blinds like gaol bars
fracture the light
that falls across the manager's desk.

Pigeons land on barbs meant to scare them,
stapled to original molding
finer than china, mottled with age.

Chalky pillars slot between windows,
fluttering bunting between them,
parading #fearless champion faces.

Second Floor:

Slates dappled
with yellow blemishes
like the stroke of Monet's brush
catches the sun the street floor misses.

Spindle turrets
of the far-off churches
cast stalagmite shadows,
attracting the eyes of the country.

Ivy Rollins

Sweet talking

Melons, golden cantaloupes. OK, sugar? he asks
hoisting one high from his loaded stall.
It's the taste of the words I come for.
That all right for you, honey?
Among the mangoes, nectarines, purple figs,
I can be darling, babe, sunshine,
cradled in speech like peaches packed in Italy.
Fifty pence, lady.
I'm sweet as black grapes, warm
as Greek sun polishing their skins,
or an apricot against hot stone.
Lovely weather, sweetheart. He winks,
a paper bag full of ripe promises,
a heart full of sweet talking;
juicy words.
Anything else, love?

D A Prince

Waiting on Western Road

At 5pm the buildings shake their people loose:
the Japanese canal with its painted-on lily pads
is an enamelled trackway,

the air is as sultry as a dark peony whose time has
         come
and I'm outside the 24/7 convenience store
sharp grit in the turnstile of commerce.

The concrete and its small thrust stage
these littered people, spreading -
they are drawn to the urban pocket park
growing its metal lamp-posts,
their bark-chip playground a citadel
with its towers and plastic slides.

Ice-cream charms are spangling the planet
with rusted atonal clangs -
and elephantine, a delivery van
goes nosing the tarmacked streets, a liner
at the dock:

petrol in the freighted atmosphere,
a curtain-wall of windows
from the clamorous 19th century
with arterial plumbing clung to its sides
like tied mountaineers, but frozen.

Rennie Parker

On Leicester Winning the Premiership

Leics-said-the-better (or Leicester, as it's known for
          short)
was traditionally a place where we didn't have much
          to be proud
apart from our self-esteem problem
and our casual hatred of Derby and Nottingham.

Our motto was "Leicester – a city full of surprises,"
which was true, because no one knew what was going
          on.

The eighties had not been kind for Leicester City:
our trophy cabinet remained obstinately empty.
We were relegated twice, Everton took Gary Lineker
and our fortunes simply nose-dived more dramatically
          than a Forest midfielder.

We rallied since then but never found the greatness inside
us, but Leicester people are flexible, so we
          supported Leicester Tigers.

And then a scandal involving the manager's son and
          other players
with some prostitutes in Thailand
caused everything to realign.
A new manager was signed
and now we're top of the premiership
and it seems to be a time
when Leicester is flourishing.

And Leicester's always been all right, like a well-kept
 secret.
We're a beacon of successful multiculturalism,
which goes way back to the textile industry,
because in Leicester, everyone's a minority.

Then you add all the bands, theatre, spoken word and
 comedy,
when we'd already given the world Englebert
 Humperdink and Showaddywaddy.
And then we found some bones of a dead bloke in a
 car park,
and he turned out to be royalty.

So now people are coming to Leicester and things are
 never dull.
It's just the shot in the arm we needed
after losing City of Culture to Hull.
So, new motto: "Leicester - not as crap as you
 thought."

And when we are knocked from our place at the top
 of the table,
we'll chuckle at the fact that, without a lot of cash,
we were able to take on Chelsea and Man U,
and whatever we might do,
or what the future might bring,
for the first time in generations, our children will say:

"I am from Leicester and I can do anything."

Rob Gee

Land locked

We live one hundred miles from sea,
dreaming of Bournemouth and Skegness,
pretending in swimming pools,
leaping off Abbey Park bridge into unknown depths
to save supermarket trolleys from drowning.

One day we went to Belgrave Hall gardens,
ate samosas, onion bhajis and apples,
licked oil and spices from our fingers,
lit candles to float downriver
and sang them off to faraway coasts.

Slug river Soar with its unjust name crawls past,
dust sticking to its surface.
We spend hours watching each mote drag by.
Moorhens give us our highest waves; hot winds fan
with an ozone ghost, faint memory of salt.

The candles foundered on debris.
Three boys came to investigate.
We're fishing for eternity, we said,
sailing to the end of the earth
where land runs splashing into sea.

I dream of folding this place
like a map, so we could step off Melton Mowbray
onto Great Yarmouth beach, walk west
from Hinckley to Towyn for cream teas
or drop by Bognor Regis for a swim.

The boys looked uneasy,
they asked if it's allowed.
We gave them all the apples we had saved.
As we left they began
bombing the candles with the cores.

Maxine Linnell

A Haiku Hike in Aylestone Meadows

Long purple loosestrife
spike, bestride crisp water mint
in Aylestone Meadows.

Scabious: so blue,
they look as if they've fallen
from a sapphire sky.

Nearby, a charred shed,
choked with nettles, darnels; starred
with wild chicory.

Long waiting lists for
leucotomies: tree surgeons
lopping poplar heads.

Aspens sadly sough,
mourn Summer's passing furlough.
Boughs torn off, laid low.

By slate-grey waters,
frost-frightened whitened willows
shedding tears of gold.

Fireweed has lost his
crimson: wispy seeds, storm–tossed,
wait to be reborn

next Summer, when long
purple loosestrife spikes again
besides blue water's

glint, in Aylestone Meadows.

Richard Byrt

The Train Man: Eddie Isaac MBE

I never knew your name
till the day you retired
but I heard your whistle
its shrill insistent sharpness
cutting through the fug of announcements
The train now standing on platform 2...
East Midlands Trains apologises for the delay
We are sorry to announce....
Market Harborough, Kettering, London St. Pancras

Eddie Isaac in your high-viz
with your peaked black cap
smartly knotted tie

Stand clear of the moving train
Will passengers on platform 3...
This train does not stop here
Syston, Sileby, Barrow-on-Soar

Eddie always ready to
welcome
urge
not in company-speak
(no 'platformed' trains for you)
but on-the-hoof banter with locals
commuters, trainspotters at platform ends
a song, a joke, a smile
while you mind the doors
keep the timetable moving

A 'Leicester legend'
you breakfast on raw eggs
fuelled by your desire to serve

Welcome to Leicester
You are so welcome to Leicester

The Queen told you
no-one will ever break your record
fifty three years working on the rail

Chill wind might blow up the platform
rain might lash along the platform
long shadows might creep across the platform
but you were there every day
always always blowing that whistle

Sue Dymoke

Time Traveller
Bronze statue by James W Butler

Outside the railway station Thomas Cook
consults his pocket watch; its hands are stuck.
He's a traveller caught in the moment,
late home from his Temperance meeting.
His son will be waiting for bedtime stories.
Marianne will be worrying –
has he forsaken the Pledge, partaken
of the demon drink at the Railway Arms,
been arrested for brawling in the street,
fallen prey to thugs or pickpockets
or into temptation with prostitutes?

She won't believe him when he tells her how
the Loughborough-Leicester trains do fly
since they ran out of steam; how hansom cabs
get by without their horses; how the road
to Market Harborough is tarred and free
of carriage ruts, alive with vehicles'
engineered roars; how he can sample
India from Chettinad to Shimla
before he's walked to Victoria Park;
how the world has shrunk since he last kissed her;
how he has played his part in this.

Jayne Stanton

Ruins steeped in history
Poem dedicated to the memory of the Leicester Abbey

the thought of Robert de Beaumont
has grown in the ground
like a shapely tree
it gave rise to the walls
of the House of God

three hundred seventy-seven years
woven with fervent prayers
steadfast fidelity
merciless time
closed the source of holiness
Henry VIII had a key

on the roads
of the abbey of Saint Mary de Pratis
among the cards of distant history
still blows the wind
born of Augustinian words and beliefs

between the walls
bathed in the past
there live the ghosts
of forgotten ideas
during the starry nights
cloaked in the mantle of memories
they go out and recall
the image of the lost Leicester

Norbert Gora

Leicester Ghost Walk

Start with a pint
at the Western Pub
on Western Road.
Hang a left out of the door
and walk down to the canal.

Stagnant water, covered in green scum
ignores the climbing frame
shaped like a pyramid,
which relishes the thought of being climbed on
by these frolicsome children
bound for the Tesco Express
next to the Bede Park column
overlooking the water,
where, through these old green railings
I spy four young oarswomen.

They have stopped rowing
under a crenellated bridge,
not far from the massive Land Registry
which is much too big to find.
That white boat moored along Castle Gardens
is made brighter by light rain,
emphasising the iron Ss
which hold those old walls over there upright.
No Ss needed at the modern Holiday Inn
which dwarfs that pub called "The Bow String".

Time stretches and curves and retreats
and I stretch and curve and retreat with it:
I glimpse me in a final exam, shaking,
leading a discussion in an old folks' home,
taking the deeds of my house to be registered,
visiting friends in their flat above the canal.

Leicester must be haunted by a million ghosts
at least. Several of them are haunting me
and I am haunted by the thought
that several of these haunters are me.

Mike Brewer

Traces
Leicester, 2015

I
Water sinks in a scrawl of plastic
wrappers. A wrecked beer-can floats
beneath a seagull's wing. Plants
overtake banks. The young
cling on, regardless. A sign in ballpoint
begs for change. The yellow cranes
stack room on room on room
here, where last year
they bulldozed the remains
of Roman lives.

II
Admire the tesserae
                    shaded, assembled
to make a god.

Gasp at the cracked paint
                    peeled carefully
from vanished walls.

The bronze pin and this clouded glass
                    survive
wasted for centuries, disused.

III
When power shifts

workers dismantle

a Roman bath-house.

They erect

a church

for conquerors.

Later,

as steeples fall

old bones are tested

for DNA

and judged to merit

both prayer and praise.

New composition.

Cash.

Court hearing.

Placards.

The slow parade

to a cathedral tomb.

Kathleen Bell

Sky Lines

When I swoop
from a white-marbled minaret
to chase sunlight hop
-scotching terraces between
Spinney Hill and Nedham Street
I loop a roundabout loop
scavenging Halal Fish & Chips
pizza crusts or spicy Sizzlerz;
duck under railway arch to dodge
a pelting from rainbowed pigeons
and emerge to knit with ululation
the multi-horizoned space
of Humberstone Gate.

By crow's flightpath
I locate a Wesleyan angel
alight on terracotta wing-tip
to keep an avian eye
along Belgrave's Golden Mile;
gorging on rubies at Ram's Jewellers
pecking at a simmering Curry Pot
with its Madras-hot aromas
of this season's saris;
I murmur with starlings over
Brogue, Sandal and Moccasin Street
skid-land at Abbey Meadows
by the Soar's river-beak.

From my perch
a Wolsey-red chimney amidst
industrial rubble and willow-herb
I out-stare that space-chrysalis
pupating a white dragonfly
until blue-feathered I launch
my own promotion
in a rattle-cheer of wings
and clear smog-rim to reach
Old John's tankard on Bradgate Hill;
from circle of black volcano teeth
a displaced skylark completes
my cat-cradle song.

Siobhan Logan

Fosse Park, After Dark

On windswept wastelands' haunted plains
Where spirit-shadows shift like sand
The concrete ghosts all hand-in-hand
Stand solemn in the evening rain.

Waiting like a shadow hound
For fox-fur orange lights to die
She crouches under sepia skies
This supermarket island town.

Trolleys waltzing in the wind
Like shrill metallic paramours
Are chained across the moonlit floor
Where sodium lights turn pale and dim.

The distant cries of car alarms
In wailing choirs remote and shrill
Come braying over sunset hills
Across the meads and streams and farms.

This graveyard grey as winter dawns
Where motorways exhale in death
Their roundabouts that curl like breath
Through ozone-winter's tepid storms.

Julia Wood

new walks in compost

she gave herself willing to compost

swapped one grey city for another
but here pushed root hands
into rich soil

here she found stiff tongues broken
down into feed and fodder
for the ground

she walks new walks here in compost

on damp earth feet
here she found flowering
of her rescuing

she found green grey decay
of herself day by day
and that's okay

she blooms here now in compost

Jodie Hannis

the field of daisies
    filled my heart
with love's ephemeral
         blooms

a misted dalliance
      veiled resonance

at earth's haze guarded
      womb

Bobba Cass

I used to have an allotment at Gorse Hill City Farm. I could reach it by walking along a footpath off Groby Road. The footpath crossed a school's playing field then still ungated. On the day I wrote this poem, the field was filled with masses of daisies.

Ratae Corieltauvorum

That's what the Romans called it.
A great city in Brittania
with a forum, bath house and Basilica.

Now the Romans are back.
This time they're warmly welcomed
and there's a petition being raised
to honour their affable leader,
Ranieri, Caesar of the city,
who restored the reputation of Leicester
with his team of fearless warriors.
The by-product is a sea of blue flags
and beaming faces pouring into the city centre
spilling over into the green of Victoria Park:
jubilation floating on an ocean of pride.
A resurgence of confidence,
an optimism vibrant as electricity;
the new King Power in town.

Andrew Button

Food Fantastic Leicester Market

"Come on, come on, one pound a bowl.
Grapes, bananas, lovely toms."
Coffee aromas from the trolley,
produce laden market stalls,
bustling, jostling shoppers.

But it's the fish that draws me in.
Red bream and strawberry grouper,
Silvery Pumphrets and Dorados
A blue without a name.
A Leicester City fish!
Salt fish, fish heads, shoulders of cod,
king prawns, headless, Kings not Tigers.

"Fat, thin, cocktail, blue,
any sausages for you?"
I'm at the magic world of meat.
Chitterlings and tripe, festive ham.
Festive? Chicken feet and turkey necks.
Faggots, three at least to form a snooker!
Pigtails? Trotters? None to buy.
No pudding and souse today.

"Onions, lovely onions, ripe bananas, come on now."
Leaves on lemons, paper on pears,
cassavas, melons, mangos,
chillies and peppers, small to large,
mild to hot, choose your colour,
from green to yellow, orange, red.
Lettuce, flat, I call them round,
red continental. Pak choi, okra, yam
and mouli, artichokes but no kohlrabi.
Why no kohlrabi?

Now, where can I find the laver bread?

Sheila Clarke

Highfields Fantasia

In,
Highfields terraced houses
concertinaed off street
or palisaded,
all night wrapped
agent orange haloed
with furtive stars
at play behind trees
patinas of trees
curlicues muezzin calls
loop into august bells
neither smother dismal djinns
false light gods pulsing
behind filigree netted windows

There,
huddled in dank kitchens
forked brows lines straighten
dwellers disrobe their disillusions
to invoke a seething alchemy
brief escape is found here
from blaring fluorescent tube lights
fatigued sombre living rooms
all blipping wiis and gameboys

They
conjure up black skillets,
tiny geysers of rice pots
fume so expectantly,
while joyfully clapping their lids
for sizzles of garlic
bangles of onions
swathes of spinach

Magic.

Carol Leeming

Kilmorie
(Victoria Park Road)

By the park a student walks
talks aloud alone,
a hand clasped to his ear.
A Toyota parks on double yellow.
Soggy dead leaves
carpet Kilmorie front.
The side gate lolls awry.
William Skillington's initials
carved in a stone tablet
above the front door
now should signify:
With Sympathy
for the spirit of the house.

The three storey house Kilmorie
Is a statement of security
Where a picture hangs in an upper room
Of a lady weaving at a loom.
Jemima Skillington looks out
To the park where children run about;
Boys in serge suits, boots and caps
Chase girls in pinafores and plaits.
A couple chat as they stroll by
A horse and trap is standing nigh.

When the Skillingtons passed away
Son and wife remained and they
Upheld eighty years of family
Gracious living in serenity.

A pop group stare out
from a poster blu-tacked
in an upper room.
Grass thrives in compost
in the guttering.
Window frames are starved of paint,
rooms with beds
are shrouded against the light.
Ivy strays in at the window.
The house cringes, screws up its eyes,
Pretends it's not still there.

Norman Harrington

A Walk with Susanna Watts
Being a Guide to Strangers

Come, take this tour with me,
ghosting Leicester, hive of industry.
Dissent runs packed as water-roads:
canals disgorging iron; lime; coal;
mills and factories deflowered
aspirations of a poor devoured.

Come, roam invisible to see
our city matron taking tea
(*Hummingbird* abetting her discover
blood-glutted histories of SLAVE SUGAR).

Penning guide book, 'for the curious,'
I noted how come every Michaelmas,
Trinity Hospital paupers graced *High Cross*
got-up as threadbare knights with loss
of dignity in rusting helmets – Gross
as sweetness bought via slavery,
            honeying our bitterest green tea.

Come, saunter past and present, linger … look …
compose a poem to place in my scrap-book,
sing of the orphan's tears, the migrant's plight,
fragile paper honing words of light.
        Turn to speak, realise I'm gone,
this woman's work? Well, it was never done.

Moths with wings brown-foxed as age
rest briefly on my guide-book's welcoming page.

Deborah Tyler-Bennett
Note: The Hummingbird was Watts and Elizabeth
Heyrick's anti-slavery magazine. Moths occur in Watts's
scrapbook, and paupers really were displayed at High
Cross.

Diary from Holloway Jail February 1907
(Alice Hawkins 1863-1946; suffragette, wife to Alfred,
mother to six)

I
6am the prison is holding its breath:
those moments before the electric lights click on.
Muscle-memory folds the two rough blankets
over the flat pillows and counterpane
while we clean and stretch out the night's cramps.
Breakfast is invariably a pint of tea and brown loaf.

Why is an equally-experienced and educated widow
and parent paid less than a childless man?
I couldn't find an answer in the Trade Unions
who didn't think of women as breadwinners.
I worked and worked but if anything happened
to Alfred, my work was worthless.

II
8am Chapel 10am Exercise Even damp
air is welcomed. Talk is banned so one
can only watch and guess another's crime.

Some have babies. Imagine being born
in a cage. Will they learn to sing?

III
11am back in cells until dinner:
haricot beans and potatoes
or pressed meat and potatoes
or suet pudding and potatoes
all with brown bread.

Refused entry when Winston Churchill
spoke at Leicester's Palace Theatre.
Alfred had to speak for me.
Without my vote, how can a politician
stand on a democratic platform?

IV
4pm Tea is a pint of cocoa
and loaf of brown bread.

I was told, "Get back to your family."
One son joined the Army, another the Navy.
Both could vote, but me, the woman
who brought them into the world,
how could I have no say?

V
8pm Lights off I stretch on a mattress
where you feel everything and ache.
Room just a degree too cold to soften
the course weaves and welcome sleep.
Fresh bruises to count in the morning.

Emma Lee

Watts Revisited
Or A Contemporary Poet's Walk Through Leicester

Visitor walk with me,
traverse this city's limits, discover
what's left of brave-faced women.

Watts and Heyrick – lives astonishing,
outside London, facing great men down,
not letting ideals wing like moths ...

Who'd be their targets now? Beggars shadow
streets, familiar insults piling,
news-media echoes, raging.

Think, circuiting Jewry Wall, or Richard's Tomb,
this city-furnace stoked radical words ...
workers' rights and creatures' rights ...

Statues stand to Richard, Thomas Cook,
a seamstress lonely at her craft.
Turmeric, tandoori spices drift
the Golden Mile's gilt thread.
Canals to Loughborough, misted grey silk,
cruisers far-cry from iron-clad roads.

Leicester's great coal-weights are gone,
High Cross glimmers. Hear re-forming heart-beats.
The scrap-book's open – empty-pages beckon.

Deborah Tyler-Bennett

Highcross

Four boys dance using windows
as their mirrors in their own private
dance Studio. As they bust
their moves all they thought about
was how good they looked.
Three girls watching
four boys dancing:
it wasn't the sun that warmed them so.
They discussed the moves
of the four fit lads
as they sidled closer to them.
Two old ladies watching this scene,
not quite understanding what
it all meant. They never saw
boys dancing in the street like this
except that day in '45 when
everybody jigged and held each other close.
What are they doing?
It's dancing my love.
Not in my world,
it's rubbish that is.
Four boys dancing.
Three girls watching.
Two old dears moaning till
one security guard
moves everyone along.

Jon Wilkins

Leicester's Gone Blue Daft!

The city's bedecked in blue,
 in honour of a wonder.
We've won the bloody football!
Which no-one thought we could, or ought to.

Giant portraits of blue-clad men
 adorn our tallest lamp posts,
  as guardians or eidolons;
some look familiar; others are mere ghosts
 haunting the city's conscience.
Should I have heard of Mr Hamer?
Am I forgetful, or is he understudy to a reserve?
What function does he serve?

Shop windows are foxy with blue insignia.
People honk car horns at random,
 as a kind of blue dementia
  has gripped this ancient town;
 a place where nothing usually happens,
  and foxes slink round furtively at night.

At the peak of this atypical frenzy,
 people dance perilously on the roofs of bus shelters,
  while policemen laugh, and shops run out of beer.
An amazing amount of litter appears.
Harried workmen try to tidy up,
 even as more rains down around them.

The Leicester City 'lifers' have been transformed by
          joy,
 entering a quasi-religious ecstasy;
while the rest of us climb on the bandwagon
 somewhat self-consciously.
We have an odd new toy, a 'Premiership', to play with,
 albeit uncertainly.
We can, perhaps must, speak with outsiders about it.

Steve Wylie

Cinema Paradiso: Matinee
For the Phoenix

Clicks of spinning projector wheels
dust from 70s' theatre seats
glittering beads of light in air
floating

sitting in most seats
enjoyed such different views
perplexed by strange subtitles
on foreign language films

clustered seats up top-left
no-one's keen to sit in
maybe broken light shade?
that didn't ever change!

Mellow, Sureshot's stage
Freedom showcase – wow!
such moving magic moments
are what Phoenix gave us

such matinees of might
such command performances
such creatures of the light
forever floating

Paul Maslowski
Note: this poem refers to what is now the Sue Townsend
Theatre on Lower Brown Street, not the Phoenix Arts and
Cinema Centre on Midland Street.

After Diwali

When they moved the big wheel from Belgrave Road
to outside Superdrug someone swung the crane
too far and sheared off the top old Priory Cross.
It sits in polythene like an unwanted parcel.
The Mercury has been and taken photos.

Last night, at the top, we were close neighbours
with a wind that froze us, wouldn't shut up.
Diwali fireworks spattered
erratic lights across the flyover, the A6 and the canal.
On the way down, Bollywood tunes; drum and bass.

Nothing sadder than the morning after. Jobs on the
        line.
A team of men in high-viz jackets and hard hats
survey the damage. A crane pulls up, from nowhere,
        dips
its hook and misses—its unseen driver adjusts the
        angle.
The big wheel attendants stand around looking at
        their phones.

Pam Thompson

The City

the city is a fickle beast
burying its past
like a gnawed bone
or pile of shite

one day it hails the King
on his way to battle
the next day it festoons his usurper
with ermine and gold
buries the skull of the usurped
beneath the bridge
that cracked it open
remembers him with a club foot
and hump

the city impatient at its confines
spills over walls
turreted gates
built to keep the hordes out
writes its name everywhere
before it goes

the castle gets a facelift
of red brick
boots through windows
timber skeleton creaks and groans
out of fear

Charles G Lauder Jr

this city

this city
is old
is older than jesus christ

this city
is young
is reborn every day at 9am

this city
is old enough
to let you move
the way you want to move

this city
is young enough
to let you be
what you want to be

Ambrose Musiyiwa

The Big Issue
For Maria

Maria, on her fold-up chair, sells The Big Issue
from her vendor spot outside the Iskcon building.
She is a YOU ARE HERE dot
in a high-vis vest of Victorian red brick wall.
She is a phoenix rising from a banking hall.

Her spine is a double-edged sword.
Her shoulders weigh miracles and dreams
against the lottery of her heritage.
Her face is a contour map of the Carpathian
            mountains
her profile as timeless as the Bucegi sphinx.
On her head lie the hairpin bends of Ceauşescu's
            Folly,
its six thousand tons of dynamite, the human cost
of moving mountains. Her eyes are Bohemian
            crystal;
they are rooms with too many views
from the windows of The People's Palace.
Her feet rock the boats of her shoes
as she cradles the Black Sea in her lap.
The folds of her skirt are rivers
feeding the Danube Delta its wealth in fish;
her layers of cardigans offer shelter to migrating birds,
Her lips support a smile to melt the Balea Ice Hotel.

This morning, Maria is no more than a chimera
of Portland stone watching over Granby Street.
She is a note through the door of Bru Coffee &
        Gelato.
Looking out from an upstairs window, Hafsa
misses Maria's *God bless you* like a lucky charm,
the twinkle in her eyes like lights gone out.
Through the ceiling speakers, Jimmy Cliff sings,

Many rivers to cross…

Maria is a ticket on a three-day coach journey.
She is Danube/Mures/Prut/Olt/Somes.

Jayne Stanton

Grand Union Canal

It is a nesting place
between towpath reeds
for a late brood
of nine ducklings
looking startled by
the traffic of boots
buggies and bikes.

It is the motorway
for a downsized
slow–down, go-back
mode of transport;
the oily slide of a
painted boat under
a booming bridge.

It is the resting place
of red-topped lager cans
a supermarket trolley
a wind-struck branch
the door of a Morris Minor
three frozen chickens
and a blue plastic bag.

It is a museum tour
of textile turrets
a factory window
bursting with buddleia
bricks like broken teeth
still-dripping pipes and
a self-sown sycamore.

It is a filter for
the catch-all of lock walls;
leaf fall and litter
coot calls and rumours
condoms and graffiti
and occasionally
bodies.

Siobhan Logan

A Canticle for Leicester

7 o'clock. Sunday morning. Dominic, my black cat,
meows like a supplicant at the stained bays.
Farther out, a navy-rig of washing strains
its odd unlikely semaphore: *t*ee-shirts, *u*nderpants, *t*owels.
   Disturbed, like an art-teacher's hair,
some low dishevelled cloud tumbles on the sky:
in the faint, myopic admissions of light
paper-boys race against addresses like orienteers,
bored and thickening husbands elope with dogs,
lost lives trespass from white ciders and cardboards of
   careers,
and God's holy anglers and ramblers pilgrim
to their scattered, county ways.
      Even in a dull citadel,
among the anonymous friezes of its griefs,
the municipal statuary of a hard-working fate,
even in a place of flat vowels and soiled surnames
unglamorous as grudgings, grimms and grykes,
on the winds of a grey river where Lear and his Cordelia
impounded their lives in the black banks, like lines
   dropped
from the play, even in such wakes on moments the
   numinous,
littering its bronze haloes like late moons.
        Semper eadem,
the motto hums. Which is to say: ever constant. Or
   always the same.
Like boredom, its pities claim. Or like the flat bread
of persistence, its unleavened resurrection in fact.

David Bircumshaw

Fourteen Eighty-five

When I think of an August long ago
Two armies on a marshy plain land field,
I see red and white majesty on show
A would-be king and one who would not yield.
A battle royal to fight, kingdom to win
Ripping households' dignity asunder,
Deaths between these kin normal, not a sin
Though all verity hidden in Stratford wonder.
Yet now buried deep within Leicester soil
The truth will out, no longer can be hid,
'Twas a man who lost his mortal coil
Not a monster of just ambition bid;
When history's victors through teeth lie
It is honesty, not just bodies that die.

Anthony L Church

West End Girl (or King Richard's Circle)

I

A visit to the Three Sisters on King Richard's Road, then
        Abbey Park
Jam jars with sticklebacks caught lurking in waters dark
Corah's knitting works belching steam and who
        knows what
Machines clicking, dyes bubbling in toxic pots

The "Rally" raw from Beeching's swathing cuts
A playground of thistle heads, rats and cigarette butts
The canal and River Soar merging and crossing
Calling echoes under bridges and pebble tossing.

II

I was ten years old when I noticed the changes start
Rows of old front doors used as hoardings broke my
        heart
Knockers left on peeling brown doors ripped from
        frames
Hiding destruction of homes, pubs, streets and lanes

A ring road they said with a new Holiday Inn
Where you could eat posh Sunday lunch then have a
        free swim
Emmanuel Church was lost - King Dick's old boys'
        school too
It was being "modernised" and you could cut straight
        through

Bowstring Bridge dismantled- the last vestige of
       Victorian glory
What's there now? A gym, new bars and flats in high
       stories
No antique centres, blue brick arches or breakers'
       yards
It's all student apartments on characterless boulevards

It seems funny now how the full circle joins
In a nearby car park there are King Richard's remains
History is lost and history is found
You can still find it if you dig around.

Ellie Henry

King Richard of Leicester

In the style of Edgar Marriott, who was responsible for many of the Stanley Holloway monologues.

I'll start with the Battle of Bosworth that happened in
      days now long gone.
Richard Three lost his life and his kingdom and
      Henry (called Tudor) had won.

Richard (Plantagenet) was born in Fotheringhay Castle,
      Northants.
Low down in the line for the throne you'd think that
      he had little chance.

So in 1452 it seemed that his fate was sealed.
But who could guess how our man could act to make
      fate yield.

When Richard was only just 8, at Wakefield his father died,
and (moving young Dick up the line) Brother
      Edmund was slain at his side.

Then Edward (the oldest) was King and heaped titles
      on Richard galore.
But in '83 he also died — of natural causes, I'm sure!

The Duke of Clarence, a brother, liked Henry for
      some unknown reason.
He drowned in a barrel of wine, accused and
      convicted of treason.

It was still quite a journey for Richard to climb to the

ultimate power.
King Edward the Vth and his brother were
        imprisoned and died in the Tower.

Richard was then declared King in 1483,
but his reign was not to be long, as you soon will see.

Now Henry comes back on the scene, having spent
        years in exile in France.
As he reached Milford Haven he threatened to give
        Richard a kick in the pants!

His English and French troops together travelled by
        day and by night,
till Henry finally decided that Bosworth was good for
        the fight.

King Richard rested in Leicester. To the White Boar
        Inn he came.
It would soon become the Blue Boar: a political
        change of name.

As his horse rode him out to the battle, his spur
        struck the Bow Bridge, 'twas said.
A woman foretold that, returning, the bridge would
        be struck by his head.

When Richard arrived the two armies were drawn up
        face to face.
A third army (that of Lord Stanley) was waiting
        nearby just in case.

Henry was Stanley's step-son, which may well have
      helped him decide
(having seen how the battle had gone) to come in on
      Henry's strong side.

That's almost the end of the story, for Richard in
      battle was slain.
His body was brought back to Leicester, where for
      five hundred years it has lain.

Archaeologists then found some bones where Grey
      Friars used to be.
But were they the bones of our Richard? We had to
      wait months to see!

A Canadian descendant was found from the
      eighteenth generation.
They tested for DNA and fever gripped the nation.

We saw on television Richard's bones laid out in line.
The presenter pointed out a curvature of the spine.

The chief archaeologist said (and there must have
      been millions who heard),
"We can say without any doubt it really was Richard III."

After another battle (though this time it was only
      talk),
Richard's bones were laid to rest in Leicester — not
      London, not York.

Colin Cook

Emergency Landing

Solid gold taps on a billionaire's jet
Mock my values
And belittle my strife

Exclusively numb
These pustules of wealth
Outnumber my living five thousand to one

But what if the unthinkable is thought?
Reason breaks the sky
And the billionaire falls

What would he find
If he put down in my town?

The sleepy Soar
Rubbing at its tired banks

A pile of bones
Both regal and diminished

And a bespectacled Italian alchemist
Quietly turning base metal into the people's gold.

Matt Middleton

The Shoemakers' Walk

Laid off after the Boer War, shoemakers
from Leicester walked to London -
later inspiring the Jarrow marchers -
lacking work and welfare, wanting a solution.

The Times reported them as *shiftless*,
and stated their *march should fail*.
They were a *menace, village idiots, restless*.
Headlines weren't their worst trial.

The men walked through Northampton,
blisters, sunburn and sprained ankles,
fed by people in villages like Lavendon,
walking on refilling waterbottles.

"The Triumph and Apotheosis of Labour,"
panels inspired by the march,
paid for by Beaumanor Hall's owner,
were installed in St Mark's Church.

Fifty thousand met Trafalgar Square.
A message's bland formality:
The King *is unable to accede to your
request*. Slow return to Leicester city.

The welfare state was built
when Amos Sherriff became Mayor.
A plaque put in the market
to remember the shoemakers.

Emma Lee

On 4/6/1905, 497 men set out from Leicester for London, led by Amos Sherriff who became Mayor of Leicester in 1922. Sophia Perry Herrick was owner of Beaumanor Hall. St Mark's Church has since been deconsecrated and is now a venue for conferences, banquets and weddings.

The Dirty Thirty

Following in the footsteps
of the Old Contemptibles
and the Suffragettes

they reclaimed their name
from a pejorative: some
loud-mouthed pundit game

for a bit of bad-mouthing
on a radio phone-in –
the Dirty Thirty. Never mind

that the figure was always
one or two to either side,
it stuck. They made it theirs.

The East Midlands: stronghold
of Spencerist collusion –
Nottingham was Scab-Land

and Leicester not much better
but for that handful
of men whose principles

defined their actions;
who came out, stayed out,
stood fast, remained strong.

Regular guys, grafters,
family men. They never
saw themselves as heroes,

shrugged off the legend
forged on the picket-lines
and given voice to at demos.

Regular guys. Miners. Union men.

Neil Fulwood

Sue and I

Before I knew the city I knew you.
Failed eleven plus. Factory life.
A single mum in Eyres Monsell,
me a kid, beginning to understand.

At bedtime I devoured your books.
You tucked me in when Babba
was on night shift and Mamma
was wrist-deep in washing-up.

You taught me adult lives
were complex, said 'it's not just
staying up late and having
your own door key.' I laughed

and felt the happy sadness
of your words. Years later
driving past Leicester prison
I thought of you, also passing

with the kids, on the way
to social services. The boy
told the bus conductor,
'that's where dad lives now.'

No-one got the joke. That day
with no baby sitter, no fame,
you begged a face behind the grille
for 50p home. The castle-prison

looming large in the boy's head,
Oxo cubes and peas for dinner.
Close to tears. My hand reaches
in my pocket for a silver coin.

Maria Taylor
Sue is Sue Townsend author of the "Adrian Mole Diaries"
and "The Queen and I."

Between two Flags and four Officers
Snapshots of Leicester across the years

A Salvation Army flag, crested, heavy with history,
raised high for dedication (of me) a month-old baby,
into the North Evington Corps.

A Midland Red bus - Scraptoft Lane to Humberstone
      Gate.
Kildare Street - Leicester Central Salvation Army
      Citadel.
Sunday School, sand trays, stories and choruses,
Anniversary celebrations; band, songsters, open air
      marches.
my grandparents (retired officers) trawling the hall
before a Meeting, smiling, greeting,
or stiffer, older, on the front row; children sent to say
      'hello.'

Visiting 4-foot nothing 'little' grandma - her
      back-to-back in Birstall Street
receiving a gift - sixpence or a bar of chocolate treat.
Filbert Street football with my father. No violence.

Running, leaping, crossing allotments, hummocked
      fields
from Cardinals Walk to Humberstone School.
Bewilderment when a scholarship pass divided our
      class
and I was labelled a 'prig' then a 'Wiggy snob'
At Wyggestion Girls' Grammar School, a 'scholarship
      girl.'

Aged 15 a move from Salvation Army to St Mary's
        Church, Humberstone
and Canon Percy Lidster (after whom the Close was
        named)
woken from his forgetful Sunday afternoon doze, to
        baptise me.
Confirmation at St Saviour's.

Nurse training at the Leicester Royal Infirmary:
night duties, discipline, blocks, shifts, strict folds of
        caps;
the "Record of Instruction and Experience"
affirmed with red ink blobs by senior staff,
pillows slips, closed edge to the door,
quilt sides equal height from the floor;
strong friendships.
A year as a staff nurse before I left Leicester.

And then, April 2016, a return
a final afternoon at Kildare Street,
as, two generations on, other retired officers
watched over Leicester Central's closure.
Memories, personal stories, names of past soldiers,
        tears;
attachments being broken, links severed, fears.
The flag, lowered
in reverence,
carried out
silence.

Dorrie Johnson (Rev'd)

Good Neighbours
With thanks to the Derby Teacher that Issued the Extra
Curricula Invite to Bali Rai

Clattering in with
          even more wide eyed intent than usual,
before I could utter
          my grunt eliciting query about the day,
she pulled herself up
          to full on, teenage, pedagogic height
and without any
          reference to recent tales of division,
informed me that
          did I know that our close neighbours
had become the first
          to achieve an equality of difference?
Laying down for me
          a tapestry woven without reliance
upon standard
          but tattered, primary coloured yarns.
For the first time in
          heavy months I felt steady handed
measuring out
          the bonds that worried parents issue
about our futures.

Trevor Wright
Bali Rai is a Leicester born writer and ambassador for the
Reading Ahead programme which aims to change
perceptions of reading

Abbey Pumping Station: Waiting

My eyes adjust to the dimness of the lair
chilled to preserve this sleeping fairground
with wheels, pumps, spokes
as intricate as gold-tinted lace.
I sense the care poured onto every inch
of metal and wood, feeding the restrained energy.
Four poised beams
pump rods bronzed with oil
wait for their moment.

Karen Powell

James Watt's Leicester walk
in which Mr James Watt, engineer (1736-1819) walks
through modern-day Leicester

How are the lichens named?
Erasmus knows. He speaks
of generative powers: mosses yield,
undo themselves, then spend and spread.

Who pinned the tree?
Bark's clipped. I dream
each twig buds iron.

Swan stretches,
and folds air
into itself, is still
on muddy depths, its feet
a hidden engine
to achieve
rest, and the look of calm.

Swan's cleanlier than man
whose waste
litters the bank
and leaves out to decay
tin, paper, cloth – all engineered,
those lost, ingenious things.

This iron bridge
that skill designed, hands made,
is brambled, grassed,
impassable. So trade has gone.

And here blank eyes
(this is what freedom means –
and, Joseph, you were wrong),
one fist raised up,
to clutch a yellow flame.

Sage Road.
The words of Paine.
Here wisdom burns.

Kathleen Bell

Incident

We moored at Lime Kiln Lock; the water
threw up reflections of trees. We tasted
tar; aftermath of a paint fire at B&Q. This picture
of a narrow-boat might have been sent from a space
in a city; here, where the ground
backed onto a college; where there were gaps in the
        sky.

He'd been walking at night, shredding a sky-
blue Rizla packet, by a canal he'd no sense of, water
unknown. Paper skins littered the ground.
Accident? He had more of a taste
for bars, for a laugh: the space
on some girl's phone waited for his picture.

We dropped down into a lock; a picture
of a future started to rise; the sky
returned; our pasts, sluiced through spaces
on either side. Amazing how water
rose then ferried us on, how a taste
for open seas was gone, like being on ground.

We could only imagine: ground
slamming up at him. Picture
it: did he stumble then fall? Taste
of the lips of a man for the first time? No sky.
Was he pushed into the water,
nudged with a toe or a heel?. Space

taken up a memory stick. Space
at the start of the 6 o'clock news, this ground.
Next day, a man with his dog, 7am. Water
stayed stumm. College kids looked on. Picture
him; yellow tarpaulin. Cops and the sky.
Like us, maybe, he had little taste

for a life that's tethered. No taste
at all for a permanent mooring. Scant space
it took to unravel a story. Sometimes the sky
has meaning; others, no clues float down. Ground
level, men in overalls scouring stones. A picture-
frame in his house slowly filling with water.

Our taste: the edges of water, its spaces.
Our home, and the pictures it sends.
Who can tell when the ground will swallow the sky?

Pam Thompson

Night Swans on the Grand Union Canal

On the canal at night,
Any colour would be dominated by dark.
Only - only the white could survive and have freedom
        to move.
Swans sleep or swim in silence.
The moonlight gives them stars for decoration.
At that moment,
I thought I was walking beside the Milky Way.

Hui-Ling, Chen

The Foundation Stones

The Corieltavi built Ratae
To protect and show strength;
To their people, to outsiders.
They laid the foundation stones.

Then the Romans came, expanded;
Built roads, straight and long.
Gave us baths and townhouses,
Leaving traces that we see today.

As the centuries passed by,
As Leircestre became Leicester,
Many people came: Anglo-Saxons, Vikings,
Normans, Lancastrians and Yorkists too.

Street by street, road by road,
The town became a great city.
Industry, creative and sporting success,
Bringing people from the world over.

Each century our city changes,
Evolving with its citizens.
The old welcoming the new,
To build the Leicester of tomorrow.

Fiona O'Neill

Recording the Snooker on the VCR

It used to be a joke to tape over recordings
of your first child's birth or your wedding.
But deep inside, if you could recognise
patterns and colours and numbers and orders,
it sort of made sense. It demolished your borders.
A few decades later, some lad at Willie Thorne's,
played in silence, his brains focused on all those balls,
a kind of meditation that made his blood pump.
People noticed his skills, the same determination
in tournaments: telepathic battles of strategy & might.
It would make Total War games look like Candy
        Crush,
since the tension in the room sometimes felt like too
        much.
But it went on and on, night by night, hall to hall,
'til the end at the Crucible, so fittingly named,
the game that made us wish VCR was still there
to record everything from such a holy night
in which the lad from Thorne's became revered
as a knight who had won in battle now
and this triumph confirmed he was king of the world.
God bless Internet streaming and digital recordings
Though milestones in our lives next to this look quite
        boring,
Selby's championship win deserves a file of its own,
a tape of its own,
a piece of memory
on its own.

Cynthia Rodríguez

The Prince of Leicester

The Romans came and raised a Fort,
Odd name, Leicester, for a stronghold of its sort,
Centurions adored this land and fair ladies,
Forests of bluebells, daff's and daisies.

How do you spell this name? I said,
He suddenly began to sing it to me instead,
He sang so long that Mother fell asleep,
Swill out that teapot and let it steep.

Summer brought shows inside the Flea Pit,
For heaven's sake, where did you sit?
The cameo's gone now forevermore,
Visions of heroes and legends of lore.

Roger and he, they ran so fast,
To slip a peek of Quatermass,
Mum said it would give them awful nightmares,
Disconcerted lads bravely confined their cares.

Off to Tech school with spanner in hand,
Later finding commerce near the golden beach sand,
In keeping, out of the sun,
English chariots in disrepair, fixed and run.

He shares Christmas crackers and pies of mince,
What unique culture has this English prince,
The pointed hat better suited for a jester,
All the same he's now our Prince of Leicester.

Cynthia Morrison

You Think

You think dreams can't be real
                              ask Leicester fans
You think believe is for stupids,
                                    you didn't see Leicester
You think work hard will not pay more
You think impossible, start from the bottom go to the
          top,
You think a worker can't be the best striker.
You think a little team can't beat a big team
                                    you didn't see Leicester
You think passion can't be bigger than business.
You think football can't make everyone happy
                                    you can't be in the present
You think tales don't exist
                              you must see this fox.

Mamadou Tall

Welcome to Leicester

this city,
a place of exits
and arrivals,
welcomes you
as you leave

Ambrose Musiyiwa
At Leicester's Railway Station, as commuters went to catch
a train out of the city, they were greeted by a sign saying
Welcome to Leicester.

Fosse Road

One – North

Under the eaves there
how we rough-and-tumbled it,
our start of life together.
How we played at house
and you pretended to cook
and I to carve
our first roast chicken.

Two – South

Here's where it got serious.
We sat out the three-day week,
hugging the gas stove for heat,
black market candles,
thanks to Rimesy from 2C, for light.
And we had to confess
we'd broken the bed.

Stuart Nunn

White Feathers in Severn Street

When Ken was 17, young women told him:
We don't want to lose you
but we think you ought to go.

Now he is home, shell-shocked, in Highfields,
they give him white feathers
outside his home in Severn Street.

He has to shut his memories
out. Shut out his memories of The Somme.
But he screams out in snatched

fragments of rats and trenches,
stenches of the lad he loved,
brain shot out beside him.

And young women still give him white feathers.
Outside his home in Severn Street.

Richard Byrt
At the outbreak of the First World War, men seen as
reluctant to enlist were given white feathers.

Memories of Goppy
Gopsall Street, Leicester

Born in the forties, one of seven, number five in fact
Always fed, clothes passed down, but don't let that
       detract,
I had a great time in the street, plenty of pals to play
Cowboys and Indians, Tick off Ground, playing out
       all day.

The war years were a bit of a blur, but everyone
       stayed cool
And when the sirens went out loud, we ran towards
       the school.
They had a shelter, dark and damp and every sound
       we'd hear
until the sirens went again and everyone would cheer.

Playing football in the road, until the copper came,
Then down an entry, in a yard, every day the same.
He never tried too hard to find us, that is for sure.
We always had a look out, then all came out for more.

The Coronation in '53, we had a party in the street.
All the neighbours did their bit, it really was a treat.
Iced buns, blancmange and jelly: all very new to me.
And later invited to watch Queenie on someone's TV.

I started St Peter's School at 3 years old, it wasn't far to go.
In fact it was only five doors up, not too far in snow.
Then it was time for Dale Senior School, again, not
        very far.
My mates who failed the Eleven Plus also joined me
        here.

In winter the snow got very deep, it nearly reached
        the ledge.
We all then went to Spinney Park and took turns on
        the sledge.
I also made a bit of dosh by clearing people's fronts.
I used to charge a bob a time, a very lucrative stunt.

When I look back on my growing years, my parents had
        it hard.
I had to share a bedroom and bed. The toilet, just
        one, was in the yard.
We had no central heating. One fire to heat the whole
        house
And inside the bedroom window, the glass was
        covered in ice.

I left and got married in '66, when England won the
        World Cup.
Worked for the local press, life was really on the up.
I don't see many of my old mates now as, sadly, most
        have gone.
But I still have my good memories. Where have the
        years gone?

Tim McCaffrey

51595

The Co-op on Uppingham Road was two quick stops
      on the bus
or a good ten-minute walk on my short legs. She
      wrote me a list,
not long, but I worried in case I got it wrong. I took
      her old bag
and they wrapped things up in brown paper with a rip
      of sellotape
jagged at the ends. The man in brown overalls took
      the stub
of yellow pencil from behind his ear, listed the prices,
      ruled a line
at the end then added up, carrying over the shillings
      and pence.
I worried that I wouldn't have enough and would
      have to choose
to leave the bread, the ham or the eggs, but I wouldn't let
      go of the jam.
They asked me my number and I still know, even though
      my phone number's gone.
There was no printed receipt spelling out the change, but a
      small coloured ticket
torn with perforations for the divi. If there were pennies
      left, I'd go to the fishmongers
next door for a twist of prawns, lug the bag down to
      Humberstone Park, sit on a swing
pulling the heads and tails off, smelling the salt, tasting the
      far-off sea.

Maxine Linnell

Newarke Fragments

1. Dulled Sevastopol cannons
slumber among wide-open
red and orange marigolds.

2. Oppressive wood: panels, cradle,
high-chair without restraints
at the Bible end of the table.
Here, Heyricks became Herricks.
Admire the portrait of a young girl,
discover it's a young boy
then notice the dog in the corner.

3. Inside the back room of Skeffington House
looking at the outside of the past
where two men lean, an implicit swagger
as they frame the central arched doorway.
Yards to their right, neither in nor out
of the floor-to-ceiling sash windows,
two women sit, between them a small child.
Side-lined, marginalised, on the edge.

4. Attic shelves of history – labelled and stacked.
Behind the racks, a row of grandfather clocks.
A dolls' house frozen in time behind glass,
another boarded up against squatters.

Karen Powell

Newarke Houses Museum
January, 2013

You step from this real Leicester street
to Wharf Street in 1946

where there are no people only taped voices:
two women in the corner shop

complaining about the weather,
that you can't get potatoes

because of the snow and even though
rationing's over it's hard to get flour.

This shop's well-stocked: Camp coffee,
Oxo, home-cured ham. A fat loaf.

Cardinal Polish that 'won't wash off in the rain'.
In the pub a man orders his usual mild and bitter,

its dregs, on the mantelpiece.
The clock's stuck at twenty five past five.

On the wall, the Victory edition
of the News Chronicle with adverts for boxing

at Spinney Hill Working Men's Club.
Soft gloves dangle from a shelf in the haberdasher's

like bagged game. Nothing's dishevelled.
Ping of goods being sent along rails.

In the pawnbroker's, jet necklaces
rest near an amethyst brooch. Golf-clubs

sidle next to a brolly. A woman's
town shoes have been placed at angles

as if they are about to off on a journey
and will not be returning. I leave when

the voices begin to repeat themselves.
Post-war, a boom time's ahead,

but no-body knew it in Wharf Street,
winter, 1946. Outside, it's still freezing.

Pam Thompson

Market Day January 1963

Night's rain gathers in tarpaulin pools
Drip drips onto wooden boards.
Distant clinking.
The light bulb man, his huge jacket bulging,
leaps onto planks, expertly twists his wrist
creating pools of light from hanging flexes,
making meagre winter warmth
for traders' hands.
The Skip Boys strain over cobbles
rumbling wheeled wicker baskets,
loaded with goods,
trailing musty Corn Exchange cellar smells.

Shoppers arrive
stilettos clicking
voices rising
traders calling,
Lineker's lovely oranges,
only a tanner for two.
Beside the Fish Market
the Pitch Boys' patter,
unbeatable bargains,
cheeky asides,
I'm not asking five, I'm not asking four,
To you, sweet'art, a guinnea, no more.

Greaseproofed sandwiches balanced on stalls
milk flecked coffee poured from flasks
emptying along with the shoppers.
Now voices echo. Vans hoot,
squeezing into line along Cheapside.
Displays disappear into boxes, into wicker skips,
along with another day's dust.
Sweepers scuffle pavement-width brushes
pushing mounting debris to the Silver Arcade bins
until the skinny light bulb man
feeds his huge jacket with waddling warmth and
clinks into the darkness.

Rosalind Adam

Leamington Street
Leicester early 1960s

The sign said
No Blacks
No Dogs
No Navies
"What does it mean?" I asked
"It means what it says," he said.
"No black what?" I said.
"You wouldn't understand."

At home I said to her
"No blacks, no dogs, no Navies."
"What?"
"It's something I saw."
"You wouldn't understand," she said.

At school I said "Sir."
I said, "No Blacks, No Dogs, No Navies."
"Quite right too," said Sir.
"I don't understand Sir."
"You wouldn't understand," said Sir.

The window that displayed the sign has gone.
The house where the window was has gone.
The street where the house stood had gone.

The sign remains.
The poster over the shop said
Breaking Point the EU has failed US
"What does it mean?" I asked.

"Too many scroungers coming here," they said.

"I've seen this sign before."
"Where?"
"In a street long dead and gone."
"They're not welcome here," they said.
"No immigrants.
"No asylum seekers.
"No more, no more, no more."

Tony Shelley
Leamington Street was demolished in around 1978 to make way for Narborough Road North.

To Leicester Where We Belong

My grandparents arrived in 1960
Carrying nothing but
A single suitcase. A wedding gift. Some cash.
My mother, a toddler, my uncle, a baby
21 days by boat. Sick for the entire trip

My grandpa made shoes for a living
Walked to Syston every day, morning and night
A five mile trip, there and back
My grandma sat by her sewing machine
Holding bits of fabric together with thread

They told us we weren't welcome here
They told us this would never be our home

They marched the streets. Put it ink.
Do: NOT COME TO LEICESTER
They waved their banners
Put posters in the shop window
No dogs. No Irish. No blacks.

My mother sang the Lord's Prayer at school every
morning,
Played the angel in the Christmas nativity
At home she would hide under the bed
Whispering verses of the Quran,
Praying she wouldn't get caught skipping mosque

They told us we weren't welcome here
They told us this would never be our home

My brothers and sisters and I
Played outside in the Blind Society carpark
Ate Asian vegetarian at school, parathas smothered
        with ghee
Our mosque was an after school club
Where the imam told us stories of times we never knew

They came marching to stir up hate
Waving flags, red, white and blue
We stood side by side in unity
Your brother, my brother
Your sister, my sister

To Leicester
Where we belong
My pride.
My joy.
My home.

Farhana Shaikh

Life in the Middle Lands

They say all life is near in the middle lands.
Soaring city of Imperial Buildings,
Spinning hills, Higher fields,
Golden smiles, Charny woods,
Rowdy hills, Brawny sons,
Bells and graves, Ailing stones,
Stoney gates, Evening tones.

They call you diverse.
A mixed sack of basmati.
Milled and sifted,
Washed and separated.
Black and white and brown grains,
And over time, some slow gains.

They say that you've seen it all,
The banished, the exiled,
The settlers, the sad to leave,
The glad to stay, the lost that never arrive.

They say that it doesn't work.
Wedged in the middling lands.
Gluing souls on the down at heel,
Low cost living in colour-blind dye houses,
Cashing chips for the layman and Walkers,
Spinning tall yarns in sweats and chops,
Thai football massaging the masses,
Shami kebab fingers for the spits and boasts.

They say you're always the same.
The more we change, the more you stay the same.
The more of us that come, the more you hold.
And it's almost over when fat man Dan sings,
Roman wraiths marching under Victorian gas lamps,
Where Queens walk to meet their Kings in secret.

They say you're the lesser of the two cities.
Leicester of too many farewells made at forked roads.
Leicester for those who were lost and bound.

Say what you will.
Our in-between-times town,
Our somewhere place,
Our middling-to-fair city.
Our middle land of always.

Irfan Master

The Patriot

Contented she stands outside number 97
in her sari, an orange glow,
silver bangles adorn her wrists,
her white hair in a neat bun,
dependent now on her walking stick
to support her ageing frame.

Her shadow clings to the red brick wall
while her grandson plays football
with his friends in the street and his England flag
droops like the ears of a basset hound
from the window above.

Her mind travels back to the day in 1972
when she left everything behind,
fled with her husband from Idi Amin,
sought shelter in Belgrave
with her uncle, aunt and family of ten.

She worked long hours in the Wolsey factory,
her husband ran the corner shop;
she had four sons: now one's a dentist,
another's a pharmacist, one drives the buses
and one runs the corner shop.

She buys her saris in the colourful shops,
peers in the jewellers' windows,
enjoys a shopping spree,
spoilt for choice on 'The Golden Mile'.

Angela Bailey

Space Blanket City

The Seamstress is warming frozen fingers
on tin-foil gold; needled by hunger
she huddles under heat-reflective shawl
stitching stories of the 'ould country'.

Thomas Cook is wrapped in gold-lamé flag:
'father of tourism' mapping the world
with Temperance pamphlets and package holidays
tucked into trusty portmanteau.

A homeless Angel, ill-dressed for the weather
in bedraggled bronze and sooty wings
crouches uncomfortably on memorial plinth
holds beaten-gold cape against the rain.

This unhelmeted king hooded by gold-leaf
is hunched against uncertain welcome;
strides like a headless Pharaoh under its peak
with Plantagenet sword and hoop-la crown.

Only the astronaut at Exploration Drive
lacks a thermal blanket for EVA walk;
hanging space-suited and gold-visored
he's barely tethered to the curve of home.

Siobhan Logan
Space-blankets are often handed to migrants on coming
ashore. In June 2016 street-artist Ambrose Musiyiwa
marked Refugee Week by draping the city's statues with
them.

A Shiver of Rain

4/8/1972 Idi Amin announced he had asked the British government to take back responsibility for British citizens of Asian origin, whom he accused of sabotaging Uganda's economy, giving them 90 days to leave the country.

Why was I shivering?
I was eighteen. It was damp in Stansted.
I was ushered onto a coach for Leicester.
Was it always going to be cold here?

I watched two raindrops. One ran smoothly,
the other forced into zig-zags around obstacles.
Like our dash to Entebbe Airport dodging
roadblocks, losing our van and contents to soldiers.

Leicester city council adverts warned
of queues for housing, schools, health services,
but what are those to a family allowed
only £50 and the clothes they stand in?

My great great grandfather was taken
by the British from India to work on the railways.
At least he knew he had a job.
A heated coach didn't stop my shaking.

Our first night was wrapped in coats
on bare boards. The dark felt warm.
My parents were up with the sun,
working for the status they had before.

I locked the image of those raindrops
in a secure safe. I studied, set up a consultancy,
mentored, networked, worked.
My safe also houses an OBE.

I've been told to go home, but where's that
to a British citizen, African born of Asian origin?
Uganda is foreign to my British born children.
I still shiver but welcome rain.

Emma Lee

As Whispered by St George

With a knife-edge of numbers/ He cuts the heart cleanly in two –
from *Crow's account of St George* by Ted Hughes

i have fallen   on the corner   i am

on the prow   of division

i am wide   eyed on my

                                        back

the exchange   building is slender

my arms are   as long as

Rutland Street   & Halford Street

i embrace this   slice   of building

with my street   -long arms   i have fallen

beneath a tower   this thin   edge of wedge

rises safe &   dangerous as

                            a lighthouse here

is the exchange   the exchange that

time demands the

                            rate @ which   lives divide

the sound of hooves clips   into the sea

-shore surf of   emergency

service sirens   the waters

of Rutland Street   & the current

114

                    -ridden straits

of Halford rub   along coast   the exchange is

a battered spit   slowly eroding in

time's cold brine   i have tripped   i have

tripped my myth's switch   fallen i   stare

@ a chess-piece   building staring

back staring down

down the decades the

centuries the   millennia the   exchange

's windows suck   in sunlight by

                    day then shed

electric-glare by   night   i will lie

                              here on

the cobbles here   on   the Tarmac   on

                the surface of

the Earth un   til   the owl in   my church's

yard stretches   her voice to touch   the ex

change's glow

                              ing glass

Mark Goodwin

On a Bus

We sat side by side, slightly
Turned away from one another,
She coughed a little,
I coughed a little.
Did not want to blow my virus
Into the way of hers.
It seems, I thought with dismay
Like we hate each other.
Only her eyes I would see
She wore a niqab, I an anorak
And a woolly hat to
Hide my faded hair, once fair.
Her eyes, I guessed, are beautiful.
For she did not look my way.
Seems, I thought with dismay,
Like we hate each other.
I reach my destination.
Will she think badly of me?
Making my way
Towards the exit, I turned
Our gazes met, I smiled,
She inclined her head
Slowly, gracefully.

Maria Ronner

The De Mont.

I wasn't born in Leicester
so I did not see the Beatles
here in 1963.
I missed Sinatra, Pink Floyd, Jon Bon Jovi
but I can still look at that stage
and see the spot where icons played
and thrilled all when they took the floor.

But my father told me of another welcome here
when fresh from France in 1940
he slept exhausted on its polished boards
extolling the comfort of that floor
(sprung for dance he would explain).
For me that hall has tales to tell
it's not just the shows I see.
That floor evokes fond memories.

Merrill Clarke

Friday Nights at Zoots
Previously the Palais de Dance in Humberstone Gate

We went out dancing on Friday nights.
The chaps stood round the dance floor proud.
The room was dark, but the stage was bright.
We went out dancing on Friday nights.
When we got home it was nearly light.
The music had played all happy and loud.
We went out dancing on Friday nights
The chaps stood round the dance floor proud.

Valerie E Dayman

Our Picasso Dish

I saw an earthen vessel, just like me,
I saw juicy zest, leave a legacy,
I saw eagle-eyes, make wavy changes,
I saw currency, promise of wages,
I saw this artist, beckoning forward,
I saw progress come, in losing our guard,
I saw best practice, develop at last,
I saw experimental, improved craft,
I saw playful art, free-form *en vacances*,
I saw inspired work, tip the balance,
I saw refined art, despite any flaw,
I saw his gift, as symmetry for all.

Fiona Linday
Lord Richard Attenborough donated his collection of
around 160 pieces of Picasso's pottery to New Walk
Museum in Leicester.

Love Poem to a Polar Bear.
After Marlowe, "The Passionate Shepard to his Love." For
Peppy, the taxidermic Fox's Glacier Mints polar bear, New
Walk Museum, Leicester.

Come live with me and be my love,
Dear Polar Bear like snow white glove
And if you need a place to sleep
I'll build for you an icy keep.

I'll sneak you past the concierge
Who sleeps and dreams of polar bears
And we can take the stairs or lift
Just like we're climbing up a drift.

And on my floor that's number two
We'll swim like divers to my rooms -
The lounge that's painted like a cave,
The arctic bathroom that I've made.

And when it's cold, you'll think it's nice
And when it thaws I'll buy you ice
And you can have your own soft seat
And a stool to rest your feet.

There in my flat I'll feed you cake,
Silver squares of frosted flake
And in my freezer, I'll keep cd -
Come live with me and be my love.

Dear Polar Bear, I'll leave those men
Who call at eight and nine and ten -
I'll be with you, my number one
Come live with me, my Polar - Love.

Lydia Towsey

You don't really get Eureka Moments

"Complicated" became "Eureka"
at 9.05am on 10 September 1984:
I saw genetic fingerprinting.

It started with a chemist's set
and sulphuric acid burns
leading to me wearing a beard.

After studies, an invite to Leicester
University gave me a lab,
a part-time technician and freedom.

to study human genetic fingerprinting,
disease diagnosis, inheritance
and evolution of genetic variations.

I proved two fifteen-year-old girls
were murdered by the same killer
but not the chief suspect.

I'd cleared a man's name.
But the killer was still out there.
We continued testing

and looking over our shoulders.
Potentially the murderer knew
where we worked, where our families lived.

The price of my insecurity was £200:
the payment made for a man
to give a blood sample for a colleague

and mask a serial murderer/rapist.
Two hundred pounds.
Until a drink loosened his tongue.

Then the trial of a man,
of forensic DNA.
If it had failed, my work...

Finally I got a good night's sleep
with news of Colin Pitchfork's conviction
on his genetic profile.

Code of a Killer was fun,
but my research asks how do more
genetic mutations get passed

from parent to child in Chernobyl
than in Hiroshima?
It will take me into retirement.

Emma Lee
21/11/83 Lynda Mann murdered. 31/07/86 Dawn
Ashworth murdered. Chief suspect was Richard Buckland,
who confessed and was proved innocent. Colin Pitchfork
was arrested after Ian Kelly admitted being paid £200 to
give a blood sample on Pitchfork's behalf April 2015, a 2-
part TV drama, "Code of a Killer" was broadcast with
actor John Simm as Professor Sir Alec Jeffreys.

And Nice One Giacomo

Tears fill the eyes of the 'Tinkerman' jester
since Spurs pulled up short, the table shows Leicester,
are champions now and they've won at a canter,
egged on no doubt by the boxer-short banter

Ranieri's boys lost just three times all season
and their ever-presents may well be the reason
why Kanté and Schmeichel, Wes Morgan and Mahrez
may shortly rub shoulders with Neymar and Suarez

While terraces rock to the B of Bocelli
its fans dream of Lineker's knickers on telly!
Foxes don't quit, dilly ding, dilly dong,
and Giacomo, pal, that's one hell of a song!

Foxes never quit is the team's motto.
Giacomo Puccini wrote the tune to Nessun Dorma,
with its penultimate electrifying B natural.

Geoff Lander
Ever-presents – ever present in the team

Valley Dreamers

On London Road
fly eyed to view
Old John's ruins
distant in braggy peak
below a city
glowers on with neon
prickly pollen beams
a whirl in gasps of traffic
no one will swallow
Lestar's rising glossolalia
hamper its wild gesticulations
neither temper its rude music
a world's there
ready to launch
its valley dreamers
long sunk deep
in a curve of earth
unbound from 'middle lands'.

Carol Leeming

The Tree of Memories

You see that patch of earth there?
Yes, that one there. The one on the right.
Can you see it now?

A tree, the Tree of Memories used to grow there.
If a big wrong had been done to you
and you felt you could not deal with the wrong on your
        own,
you went to the Tree of Memories
and you spoke of your grievance.

The Tree listened.
And if your wrong was big enough,
The Tree called out to others
and it made your voice big.

If the wrong that had been done to you was not corrected,
the tree remembered.
And when you passed by
on your way to the house of trees,
and when you went past the house of meetings
or past the wishing well,
the Tree of Memories told you it remembered
and it told you to stay strong.
It told you to keep doing what you were doing
and that one day
the wrong that had been done to you
would be corrected.

And if you had a friend
and your friend was being treated in a most appalling
        way,
you gave The Tree to your friend
and The Tree of Memories became your friend's tree.

Yesterday someone cut down The Tree.
They cut it
as if it was theirs to do with as they liked.

But,
when you cut the Tree of Memories,
what happens
to all the wrongs it was trying to right?

Ambrose Musiyiwa

from Sun-Fall & Tools, a Watermead Park, a Charnwood, a May 2011

> laid out in the sun
> on the turf on a roof
> of a locked-up birdhide
> beside an old gravel-pit

where perhaps once
the bones of a mammoth were found

I heard hard very solid boys approach

there was the ratchet of a
bike's back-wheel-spr
-cket & the wet
haaarrk tpuuuhh

of a lad gobbing

they were below me and couldn't see
I was there listening

to the gravel & silk
of their young masculine
Leicestershire accents

these were liminal-lads
off an estate on Leicester's
northern rim

I heard one say why

the birdhide I hid on top of was

        locked

        but as is
        the way with

        memory

        I can only say
        that I think

        the birdhide was once
        the site of a fire

        that by byelaws
        should not have been

        lit

Mark Goodwin

Highfields

The shuttered synagogue at the end of my street
hugs its solemn bricks against the cold.
Ponderous façade amongst the dark and oily trees.
While beggars contemplate defeat
all along the sheltered wall of the soup kitchen
            readying
to open up its doors across the road

And Ahmed waits in patient stillness ten feet from his
            door
for his dancing little daughter
to gather up her dropped madrassa bag
like a stitch fallen from a careless needle.

Long learning
Day after awkward day
Clinging at the shawl upon a grandmother's shoulder.

There's a crescent moon rising over Highfields
Catching in the arms of a sentinel lime.

And McKenzie every afternoon rides his daddy's hip,
easy on their bicycle,
along the dusty pavement.

A church bell rings.
There's a song from half the members of a Slovak
            gypsy band
Freckled girls in tracksuit tops and skirts down to their
stardust glitter sandals

In perfect counterpoint
Walking as they sing.
Past a crate of plantains.
A spilt can of lager
A fallen school sticker
One old chair
A broken toaster rusting in a beam of taxi light.

And lying by a lamppost is yesterday's paper.
The vigil candles stuttered in the breeze
That I will remember.

And on Connaught Street the token of a poster in a
window saying, 'I have a dream.'
Every dream, every night.

Yevgeny Salisbury

Foxes on the Couch

Stoneygate: Hampstead of the Midlands.
Unfurling leafy roads, mind-altering:
Francis Street, seaside echo shops,
Victoria Park smothered in knowledge.

The ghosts of Barclay Street, Narborough,
knocking on your door. The Buddhist Centre,
behind the Cathedral, asking for you to enter
Vardy's mental continuum, scoring.

A taxi driver in Berlin now knows Leicester.
Larkin lived around the corner from you,
everyone does, lying back on their couches,
whispering you Freudian dreams, for a fee.

Jason Lee

Why I am proud of Leicester

Not too much to love --
a bit workaday, plain --
but when push came to shove
it voted Remain.

D A Prince

When Leicester becomes a republic

When Leicester becomes a republic
What will happen
To the dead king?

Will his tomb
Be dug up
And his bones sold
To Yorkshire
Least the bones,
Like oil,
Provide a pretext
For war?

Ambrose Musiyiwa

Fishpaste
A tribute to the small presses of Leicestershire

Press well the kippers, and use the New Broom,
To sweep clear the sawdust, from the Brown House's
       room.
Add Sweet Cherry marmalade, to taste for the child,
And a pinch of Fox Spirit to temper the wild.
Mix it up well, while singing to Orpheus' song,
Tap your pen to the tune, as Troubadour play along.
Add a bright dash of colour from Dahlia's bud,
If you can Factor it in, a twist of Fiction is good.
Cover with Matador's flag and leave by its self,
Once finished, bind carefully and place on a shelf.

Penny Jones
Fishpaste was a set of poems printed on postcard by one
of Leicester's first small presses: the Pandora Adana
Letterpress. When asked why it was called Fishpaste, one
of the press's owners, Rigby Graham stated, "Because no-
one quite knew what would be in it." Under his
pseudonym Norman Pinley he had also stated, "A thing
like that could only emanate from those oafs in Leicester."

Hear the Roar

beer and banter in the bar
a happy mix of us and them
then stroll to the stand

red green and white flags excite the air
the opening riff of Smoke on the Water
overwhelmed by chants of "Tigers Tigers"
as the players emerge

kick, catch, pass back, race forward
towards the far line
power and pace sets pulses racing
crunching collisions slow the flow
and cause the crowd to gasp

whistle blasts keep some control
lost tempers or disobeyed rules
mean yellow cards and the Sin Bin
for ten minutes of regret

clumsy play leads to scrums
eight against eight
physiques that women admire
and men aspire to
push to win the ball
rucks, mauls, penalties, lineouts follow
momentum grows as points build.

At the final whistle
combatants shake hands like old friends
fans mingle and celebrate:
our boys, our warriors
our Leicester Tigers

Liz Byfield

"Are you from DMU or Leicester Uni?"
(after John Osborne)

She asked me "Are you from DMU or Leicester Uni?
Because I've seen you around,
but the other day when on Queens Road
I happened to see you from afar."
Flattery aside, it made me wonder
what was she exactly doing on Queens Road,
knowing that the people from West End
believe Victoria Park is an ocean.
I wonder how did she manage to get lost,
fall asleep on the bus and wake up
in the south side of town?
Maybe her grandma lives in this other country
named Clarendon Park?
So she goes to visit and feed her,
every once in a while.
Spends the afternoon dusting off doilies
in nan's Montague Road semi-detached.
She prepares tea and bakes scones
with gluten-free flour
because nan's indigestion
has recently gone too far.
In fact, maybe the time she saw me
she was coming back from the Infirmary
to collect some of nan's belongings
before a week in observation.
"Get me my knitting bag, love,"
she asked her.
"I need to finish these cosies for Easter,"
but her grandchild was wondering if Glory Sunday

        would see her
and if Good Friday would actually be very, very bad
as the tumour, they said, had extended from stomach
        to spleen.
So that day, although her brain was elsewhere,
in a millisecond she noticed me
and maybe wondered all these things,
better or worse,
and fantasised about my studies and bearing.
So to her question I replied "I study nowhere,"
but then I thought, "I study people.
I study everywhere."

Cynthia Rodríguez

Shedding
For Janet

wearing the warm wind   wearing away

at me wearing at   some   way the oldest
rocks   hornstone printing into   my back

-skin the wind's   warm torn voices   roll
in my ears guttural but spacious rush hush

weaving my brain 's surface to rippling salt
y see the wind's   empty shiatsu hands   loll

my head my   face   a dish to the sun   fill
ing with light's collected distance Leicester

in its bowl below   Bradgate high   g round
as majestic as Sydney today   soft September

glints   a mother-board processing people   my
eyes close over now wearing   the warm wind

tears on   my skin tears   at my skin the wind
rooting up my nostrils rips   off my face over

& over &   over again my mask   stretched
with   the wind my skin   a flapping flag ever

lengthening the   wind copies   my expressions
over   &   over carries   copies of my   miles

down an old land copies of off my face my
bones & meat & guts all bl own over rove

out & out & out a cross hope's vast digesting
space like leaves leaving the oak trees face

    flung to   air all   ways

Mark Goodwin

Yakking

So there's this toddler, right,
about three years old and he's
with his nan and got this big loaf
and he's yakking it, slice by slice,
over the railings (spikeless) into
the river for ducks. This other
toddler she comes up, with her nan,
and he gives her some bread, and the
nans start chatting and the little girl
starts yakking at the ducks below who
are quacking like crazy, scattering,
'cos they're being pelted by the bread
and fighting each other and the kids
are laughing and screaming and the nans
keep talking and the girl's climbing,
hauling herself up with tough little hands,
reaching the top with an elbow, legs
swinging through the railings and the nans
are still yakking and the other elbow's up
and now she's balancing on her soft
belly, the ducks still looking pretty
pissed and flapping and the boy's laughing
and, finally, her nan looks and it's slo-mo
to the kid whose head is just about to go
down and the ducks stop clacking
and the other kid shuts up and...
....the nan's strong hands go round a leg
grab the collar – and everyone breathes.

Marilyn Ricci

King Lear, second-hand
(we two alone will sing like birds i'th'cage)

out of old mythologies

On a creaking table, from better days,
thinking on OS maps, and picture frames,
I lay down here this old, foxed coat
like something off the peg of Philip Larkin
as he looked out from a high, attic window,
as if through the hushed breadth of a library,
over London Road, and Clarendon Park,
and, no longer singing further off,
all the dead birds of Leicestershire.

David Bircumshaw

Leicester is homeland

We are citizens without a homeland,
Hunted like birds without sky,
Taught how to cut our wings,
Cage our love inside us,
Love is sin - not forgiven,
Freedom of speech is shame,
We are immigrants on all maps without addresses,
Travellers, paperless, without passport,
Bodies without coffins,
We are slaves of time,
Sell us all governor and get the price,
Here here, stop your journey here, stop your
        suffering, exile and grief.
Welcome Leicester has revealed to us what it means: love,
        peace
and homeland.

Malka Al-Haddad

The Art of Winning

Here's to the art of winning, to the team
no more the underdogs nor Little Leicester.
Here's to dreaming the impossible dream.

GET IN THERE!!!! IT'S A GOAL!!!! on live stream,
flying pigs foxing the bookmakers.
Here's to the art of winning, to the team

with spirit, the game in their bloodstream
winning the hearts of the naysayers,
keeping alive the impossible dream.

Here's to the city embracing the meme,
turning it blue in a surge of King Power.
Here's to the art of winning, to the team

at Vardy's kitchen party. Here's to the screams
of the stars in our eyes; nessun dorma
for Leicester, the birthplace of dreams.

Here's to Ranieri's We Do Not Dream scheme
from pizza to Salt & Victory flavour.
Here's to the art of winning, to the team
and the city, to living the dream.

Jayne Stanton

Fearless Lestah
The Historic Victory Night Leicester City Football Club
Wins the Premiership League 3 May 2016

This night our sky looked
liked it had if been punched
bruised sore with despondency
my own mood was mardy far
darker than clouds grumbling
over Lestah city while I fumed
Chelsea FC our Damocles sword
had played gash to half time
Tottenham Hotspur scurried
across the field like whitehead ants
threading before stuffing balls
past a flailing Chelsea keeper
twice I roared with curses blue
so fierce crackling with despair
I viciously willed our fearless foxes to victory
But how could it happen now…

Oh yer date I'd gorra it wrong!
like a biblical lazarus
or snow white waking up
filmic vampires or zombies
suddenly dancing darkly back to life
like an inert frankenstein
twitching into life to sit bolt upright …

Chelsea had come to Lestah's rescue!
Glory be it was in the second half
players Gary Cahil Eden Hazard
their hallowed names will now
be mouthed down the ages in
ribald songs of legend by lestah folk
as to how they made our… premiership
fairy tale title dream come true so

From the heart our valley city of
Lestah folks unleashed hues and cries
vivid rainbow swell of honking cars
woops of wails joyous exuberances
breaking out like a rash across the city
For our football champions of Lestah
Dilly Ding Dilly Dong rings Raneri's rhyme

The whole world now knows   m'duck
The whole world eagerly awaits… m'duck

Carol Leeming

The Recusants

Leicester Guildhall, one autumn night in 1605. King James I has excommunicated Catholics. The King's Men are touring. Tonight they are performing in Leicester. Shakespeare's father-in-law has been hung, drawn and quartered for his Catholic activities. Another Catholic revolutionary, Robert Catesby, leader of the Gunpowder Plot, who is biding his time until 5 November, decides to visit Leicester's Guildhall for an evening of theatre by his cousin, William Shakespeare, who is previewing a new work, entitled "Macbeth".

Robert Catesby

"A worthy play, my cousin Will selects
The madness of a Scottish King as plot;
But, faith, your will, a swan with two loose necks,
Equivocating, ties itself in knots.
Our families hath been branded traitors, while
You wear your truths like ladies' gloves.
A nation that confuses faith and state
Divides its people, doth not earn our love.
Look to your coat of arms, sir, 'Non Sans Droit',
Let hist'ry show that gentle Shakespeare pranced
In hose while others fought for Cath'lic rights
To blow the Scot back to his native land.
'The Kings Men' aptly names your business,
I never saw a show more false than this."

William Shakespeare

"Faith, would you die for goodness, live for crime?
Why should we kill when poverty and plague
Are swifter than the wrath of humankind?
No soul hath ever died of watching plays.
'Tis true, I am a common tanner's son,
But one whose conscience stretches leather-like.
Mine is the art of concealment, kinsman,
As hard the hammer, soft the mallet strikes.
The fox, a hunted wretch Justice begot,
Knows many things, the hedgehog one big thing.
I take my lead from lovers who will not
Let right and wrong prevent their playmaking.
Let them hang, draw and quarter my poetry,
Display my words on gates for all to see."

Kevin Fegan

Shakespeare at the Guildhall

1594 "King Leir", a play featuring a king with three
daughters the youngest of whom is Cordeilla, published
around the time Shakespeare's company visited Leicester's
Guildhall; 1610 "King Lear" published.

Cordeilla knows her sisters will say whatever
Leir wants to hear, falsely thinking flattery
will advantage them, unable to see
short term gains make for long term disaster.
Leir calls the tune to his narcissistic dance.
Cordeilla's ears open to the discordant
undertones so he makes her his scapegoat.
Isolated, sneered at, she's sent to France.

I stand in the Lord Mayor's ornate Parlour,
Here Shakespeare learnt of a Leicester king, Leir,
who only welcomed two of three daughters.
Myth became play. I stray. I face my fear.
I'll fail this. I was my mother's mirror
to reflect back love, and flatter for her
credit. I wasn't allowed to falter
away and become my own director.

Leir lost a kingdom to learn his lesson.
Elderly and needing care, he retreated
to Cordeilla when family rejected
him. She saw a humble man able to listen.

I sense echoes in this historic room.
They'd been published: I would read my poems
in a strange city where I'd first felt welcome
and where, for the first time, I had a home.

At the Guildhall, Shakespeare read the Leir play,
which seeded subplots, grew like rosemary.

At the Guildhall, I finally faced my fear.
I can cut my past, my future is here.

Emma Lee

Charivari

Uncaged for its unique day the carnival
clatters from park to street to park again,
concatenates reggae, calypso, shrill whistles,
snubs gangsta, ragga, hiphop, house.
'Wun be sin dead there, man.'
Adjusting doors for new-laid carpets,
I add a cross-ply of planing,
The rough music eclipsing the white noise
of cars and sirens: sirens and cars.
I remember that once, each day was a charivari,
the street a jostle of competing cries:
'Best blacking in the whole world'
'Blacking good enough to eat.'
Mr. Punch jousting with Judy,
Jack Ketch and the Grand Signor;
'Who'd be plagued with a wife...'
'Jack Ketch is dead - I'm free;
I do not care now, if Old Nick
Himself should come for me.'
of broadsheet sellers and balladeers;
'Young Morgan was a rattling blade,
          No lad of better courage....'
of dark, grand tumults like those
surging up Holborn-hill to the game deaths
on the gallows of Tyburn.
'Our peepers are hid from the light,
The tumbril shoves off, and we morrice...'

Paul Lee

Home

I know this city like the back of my hand
I know its streets,
its shops,
its pubs,
its cafes.

I know the market stalls
the ones with the freshest fruit
and the most potatoes for a pound.

I know this city
and it knows me.
I have spent afternoons in museums,
hands pressed together in church,
shoes taken off in gurdwaras.

I have sought shelter from the rain
in mosques,
in temples,
synagogues.

People say, "You don't sound like you're from
        Leicester"
What does that sound like to you?

To me, it is a dialect rich with sounds
with nuances and differences
and the familiar cadence
of home.

Maisie Rose Bamford

Contributors

Rosalind Adam is a Leicester girl, born and bred. She was a teacher before writing got hold of her. Now she is a writer with many short stories, articles and three books for children published. Her most recent publication is "The Children's Book of Richard III."

Malka Al-Haddad is an Iraqi academic who has lived in Britain since 2012. She is a member of the Union of Iraqi Writers, Director of the Women's Centre for Arts and Culture in Iraq and an activist with Leicester City of Sanctuary.

Maisie Rose Bamford is an English Literature graduate living in Leicester. She will be continuing her studies with an MA in Modern Literature, further exploring her love for modernist and postcolonial poetry and prose.

Kathleen Bell has published in a wide range of journals and is the author of the chapbook "at the memory exchange" (Oystercatcher, 2014). She is one of the editors of the anthology "Over Land Over Sea: poems for those seeking refuge" (Five Leaves, 2015) and lectures at De Montfort University.

Michael Brewer has had poems published in several magazines. His villanelle "How to Ride a Penny Farthing" appeared in a collection celebrating the start of the Tour de France in Yorkshire. Over the last seven years he has been a regular open mic performer at the Y Theatre in Leicester.

Liz Byfield has a life-long love of poetry but only recently began writing her own poems. She has taken part in open mic sessions in and around Leicester and has performed on the foyer stage at Curve theatre and at the Radnor Fringe Festival.

Richard Byrt has lived and worked in Leicester since 1986. He is a keen participant in local Pinggg…K! Shindig and Word! poetry events. Richard's first poetry collection, "Devil's Bit" (De Montfort Books, 2015) was commissioned by Upstairs at the Western Pub Theatre.

Bobba Cass is a gay grey poet born in Seattle, Washington, USA, but living in Leicester/shire since 1973. He organises a monthly spoken word event, Pinggg…K! which celebrates the metrosexuality of verse. He is a member of the People's Arts Collective, Leicester and helps convene Choral Poetry for Leicester.

Leicester-born political activist **Anthony L Church** writes plays, short stories and poems. He is principal writer for the Loughborough-based Stage Left Theatre Workshop, for whom he also acts.

Merrill Clarke took up writing poetry when he retired a few years ago. He attends poetry workshops and open mic events around Leicester and occasionally performs his own poems.

Sheila Clarke started writing poetry after she retired having been attracted by attending poetry classes at Curve,

Leicester. Her main motivation is whether she will be able to do it. She still enjoys trying.

Colin Cook was born and brought up in Leicester. He spent nearly all his live there, apart from two years in National Service (where he learnt to type) and three years at university. Consequently he's seen many changes in the city, not all of which he's liked.

Valerie Dayman is happy with a book in her hand, now she has a pen as well. Friends and family would like her to write about her life and, maybe, one day she will: when she's not too busy living it.

Sue Dymoke is Reader in Education and National Teaching Fellow at the University of Leicester. Her second full poetry collection is "Moon at the Park and Ride" (Shoestring Press, 2012). Her research focuses on poetry pedagogy, and other publications including "Making Poetry Happen" (Bloomsbury, 2015). She blogs at suedymokepoetry.com

Neil Fulwood is the co-editor, with David Sillitoe, of the anthology "More Raw Material: work inspired by Alan Sillitoe" (Lucifer Press, 2015). His debut collection, "No Avoiding It", is forthcoming from Shoestring Press.

Rob Gee has performed over 2000 shows worldwide and is sometimes sent into schools as a warning to children. Poetry slam victories included The Edinburgh Slam, BBC2's Why Poetry Matters Slam, The Arts Council's Lit

Up Slam and the Orlando Poetry Smackdown. He's won over 15 international awards for his solo shows.

For 15 years **Mark Goodwin** has lived afloat on Leicester's northern rim. Much of Mark's work is about experiencing place. He contributed to "The Ground Aslant an anthology of Radical Landscape Poetry" (Shearsman, 2011). Mark's collection "Steps" (Longbarrow, 2014) was a category finalist in the 2015 Banff Mountain Book Competition.

Nobert Gora is 26 years old and a poet and writer form Poland. He lives in a little town of Góra, Poland. Many of his horror, SF and romance short stories have been published in his home country. He is also the author of many poems in English language poetry anthologies around the world.

Jodie Hannis is a Leicester-based writer and performance poet finding no end of words and inspiration in her adoptive city. She performs regularly with the House of Verse and Anerki collectives and is a regular contributor to The Grade, Everybody's Reviewing and soon-to-be print publication Great Central.

Norman Harrington worked for 10 years in the family shoe making business, the former warehouse of which is in Leicester's Cultural Quarter. The lure of open air made him change occupations and Norman worked on a nursery and learnt to grow roses. He has written 500 poems.

Hui-Ling, Chen was born in 1976 in Taiwan and is in the

second year of a PhD in education at De Montfort University.

Penny Jones is a writer from Leicestershire. Her work has been published in "Over Land Over Sea: poems for those seeking refuge" (Five Leaves, 2015), in AdHoc and for National Flash Fiction Day. Her first short story is published in an anthology from Fox Spirit Books (2016)

Charles G Lauder Jr was born and raised in San Antonio, Texas and has lived in the UK since 2000. His poems have appeared internationally and his pamphlet "Bleeds" was published in 2012 by Crystal Clear Creators. Most recently he was highly commended in the 2015 Poetry Society Stanza Competition. He is the Assistant Editor for "The Interpreter's House".

Emma Lee has published three poetry collections, "Ghosts in the Desert" (IDP, 2015), "Mimicking a Snowdrop" (Thynks, 2014) and "Yellow Torchlight and the Blues" (Original Plus, 2004). She was co-editor for "Over Land Over Sea: poems for those seeking refuge" (Five Leaves, 2015). She also reviews and writes short stories, one of which, "Someone Else's Wallpaper" is in "Lost & Found: stories from home" (Dahlia Publishing, 2016)

Jason Lee is Professor of Culture and Creative Writing at De Montfort University and Head of the Leicester Media School. The author/editor of 20 books, his work has been translated into 16 languages. His latest poetry collection is "Fire Lines" (Eyewear, 2016). Palgrave is publishing two of his critical books "Sex Robots" and "Child Sexual Abuse and the Media". His latest novel is "Spit Roast" (Roman, 2015).

Paul Lee (1952-2011) was born in Leicester and published a poetry collection, "The Light Forecast" (Original Plus, 2005). "Us: who made History" (Original Plus, 2012) was published posthumously. He also wrote short stories and reviewed for "The Journal."

Carol Leeming FRSA is a polymath: an award-winning writer, playwright, published poet, performer, director and filmmaker. Her creative work has been broadcast on BBC Radio 4 and BBC Radio Leicester and shown at regional theatres. Carol is a successful singer/songwriter, composer and musician and has received international acclaim. https://daretodiva2000.wordpress.com/

Maxine Linnell is a writer, creative writing teacher, editor, mentor and Leicester-lover. She was born here too long ago to remember, and lived away for many years. Now she intends to stay, though we never know. Her poetry collection comes out with Soundswrite Press in 2017, and she has six published books.

Siobhan Logan's poetry and prose collections, "Firebridge to Skyshore" and "Mad, Hopeless and Possible" are both published by Original Plus. Her digital narrative "Philae's Book of Hours" is published online by the European Space Agency. She teaches Creative Writing at De Montfort University.
http://siobhanlogan.blogspot.co.uk/ @siobsi.

Paul Maslowski spend many happy hours writing poetry in and around Leicester, performing at Word! on occasions. He now lives in Market Harborough - still Leicestershire - and is now a member of Rutland Poets.

Irfan Master is the author of "A Beautiful Lie" (Bloomsbury) which was shortlisted for the Waterstone's Children's Book Prize and Branford Boase Award for debut authors. He recently had a radio play published, "For the Love of Something" in Hidden Stories - an illustrated collection of writing specially commissioned by Leicester University and a short story in "Lost and Found: Stories from Home" (Dahlia Publishing, 2016) an anthology of original and diverse stories on the theme of home by Leicestershire writers. His forthcoming novel for young adults "Out of Heart" will be published in 2017.

Matt Middleton is a poet and short story writer who lives in Leicester, where he works as a plasterer.

Cynthia Morrison BA resides in south Florida where she is a writer, artist, stage combat director and an award-winning playwright. She is a graduate of the Burt Reynolds Institute for Film and Theatre. Her plays have appeared off Broadway in New York, Washington DC and London.

Ambrose Musiyiwa facilitates CivicLeicester, a community media channel and is author of "The Gospel According to Bobba," "The Gospel According to Sheila" and "The Gospel According to Carol."

Rennie Parker is from West Yorkshire, but she lived in Leicester briefly and began her publishing career in 1987 while attending workshops at Vaughan College (Leicester). She's performed at Shindig events, held at the Western, and also learnt printmaking at Leicester Print Workshop.

Karen Powell lives in Leicester and has an MA in Creative Writing from Nottingham Trent University. Her poetry has been published in "Soundswrite 2015: an anthology of contemporary poetry", and various magazines including "The Interpreter's House", "Ink Sweat & Tears" and "The Lake".

D A Prince lives in Leicestershire and London. She has two collections from Happen*Stance* Press: "Nearly the Happy Hour" (2008) and "Common Ground" (2014) which won the East Midlands Book Award 2015.

Cynthia Rodríguez is a writer, translator, filmmaker and performer, transmitting stories and messages from different points of view. Born in Monterrey, Mexico, she is currently based in Leicester. Open mic performer for Anerki, Find the Right Words, Word!, Pinggg...k! and more. Author and Illustrator of zines "Santa Belleza", "First Crush" and "The Epic of Giddy Legs."

Ivy Rollins is 24 and lives in Leicester with her husband. She studied Creative Writing at the Northampton University where she developed a love of writing. She is now a primary school teacher where she gets to test out her children's stories on her Year 3 class.

Yevgeny Salisbury is a poet, novelist and artist who few up on the island of Anglesey in a remote farmhouse insulated with books. He now lives and works in Highfields, Leicester. He is a former President of Leicester Writers' Club and a regular performer with the UK Poetry Brothel.

Farhana Shaikh is a writer, publisher and journalist born in Leicester. She edits "The Asian Writer" and manages Dahlia Publishing. Farhana lives in Leicester with her husband and their two children. She tweets about books and publishing @farhanashaikh.

For more than two decades, **Tony Shelley** has kept regular diaries and journals. He is a life-long socialist.

Muir Sperrings discovered writing eight years ago when she wrote a eulogy in memory of her Aunt - it was a poem. Since then she has been on a couple of writing courses taking inspiration from the surrounding countryside and city. Opposite her converted Victorian flat on the edge of Leicester city is an acre plot left to the wildlife that inhabit it: foxes, badgers and various insects, a veritable stimulus. Poems are her first love, but she has turned her hand to short stories as well.

Jayne Stanton lives, works and writes in Leicestershire. Her poems appear in various print and online magazines. A pamphlet, "Beyond the Tune" is published by Soundswrite Press (2014). She blogs at jaynestantonpoetry.wordpress.com and tweets @stantonjayne.

Pam Thompson is a poet and university lecturer based in Leicester. She is one of the organisers or Word!, a spoken word, open mic night at The Y Theatre in Leicester. Her publications include "The Japan Quiz" (Redbeck Press, 2008) and "Show Date and Time" (Smith-Doorstop, 2006) and "Hologram" (Sunk island Publishing, 2009). She has been widely published in magazines, such as "The North," "Antiphon," "The Rialto," "Mslexia," "Magma," "The Manchester Review" and "Under the Radar" and has been successful in poetry competitions, the most recent being as winner of the Judge's Prize in the 2015 Magma Poetry Competition.

Lydia Towsey has appeared at the House of Lords, London's 100 Club and Roundhouse, amongst others, and in 2014-15 toured "Three the Hard Way" http://www.3hardwaypoets.wordpress.com/. Featured in "Hallelujah for 50ft Women" (Bloodaxe) and "10 Poems about Knitting" (Candlestick), her collection "The Venus Papers" is published by Burning Eye.

Jon Wilkins has always wanted to write. No evidence remains of his childhood writings. He taught for 20 years and then worked in Waterstone's for 10, though he still loves books. He is currently taking an MA in Creative Writing at De Montfort University.

Julia Wood holds a Master's Degree in Continental Philosophy from Warwick University and has published a non-fiction book, "The Resurrection of Oscar Wilde: a Cultural Afterlife" (Lutterworth Press, 2007) along with numerous academic articles about Oscar Wilde and Lord Alfred Douglas. Her distinctive Victorian style and passion for the era has received extensive media exposure. She has written four novels, all paranormal-themed. She enjoys the poetry of Sir John Betjeman, Keats, A E Houseman, Alfred Douglas and Oscar Wilde.

Steve Wylie was born in Glasgow sixty years ago. His mother was just passing through. He should have been born in Edinburgh. He came to Leicester to work for the now defunct Marconi Radar Systems and has been here ever since. He is well-known in Leicester poetry circles.

Acknowledgements
Some of these poems have been published previously as follows:

Henna On Her Hands Dawn Bauling in "Shippen" (IDP, 2014)

On Leicester winning the Premiership Rob Gee broadcast on BBC Radio 4

Shedding Mark Goodwin first published by "Stride" magazine and included in "Back of a Vast" (Shearsman, 2010)

From Sun-Fall & Tools, a Watermead Park, a Charnwood, a May 2011 Mark Goodwin first published by "Shadowtrain" magazine and included in "Layers of Un" (Shearsman, 2012)

The Shoemakers' Walk Emma Lee in Proletarian Poetry

A Shiver of Rain Emma Lee in Well Versed, The Morning Star

Shakespeare at the Guildhall Emma Lee in New Walk Magazine (UK) and "When I Move" (Silver Birch Press, USA, 2016)

Charivari Paul Lee in "Us: who made History" (Original Plus, 2012)

her green lap Paul Lee in "The Light Forecast" (Original Plus, 2005)

Secular Hall Paul Lee in "Us: who made History" (Original Plus, 2012)

Highfields Fantasia Carol Leeming in "Out of Bounds: British Black and Asian Poets" (Bloodaxe, 2012)

Valley Dreamers Carol Leeming in "Out of Bounds: British Black and Asian Poets" (Bloodaxe, 2012)

Grand Union Canal Siobhan Logan in "Soundswrite 2011"

this city Ambrose Musiyiwa in The Leicester Mercury

When Leicester becomes a republic Ambrose Musiyiwa in "The Gospel According to Sheila"

Newarke Fragments Karen Powell in "Expresseumpoetics".

Sweet talking D A Prince in "Other Poetry" magazine (August 2002)

Yakking Marilyn Ricci in "Rebuilding a Number 39" (Happen*Stance*, 2008)

To Leicester Where We Belong Farhana Shaikh in "Do Something" (Factor Fiction, 2016)

The Art of Winning Jayne Stanton written during a poet-in-residency at Bru Café and Gelato, Granby Street, Leicester during the Leicester Writes Festival

The Big Issue Jayne Stanton written during a poet-in-residency at Bru Café and Gelato, Granby Street, Leicester during the Leicester Writes Festival

Time Traveller Jayne Stanton written during a poet-in-residency at Bru Café and Gelato, Granby Street, Leicester during the Leicester Writes Festival

A Walk with Susanna Watts Deborah Tyler-Bennett in "Friendship's Scrapbook: Poems by Deborah Tyler-Bennett and Jayne Stanton" (University of Leicester, 2015)

Watts Revisited Deborah Tyler-Bennett "Friendship's Scrapbook: Poems by Deborah Tyler-Bennett and Jayne Stanton" (University of Leicester, 2015)